Homestyle Elegance

otis marston's california cuisine

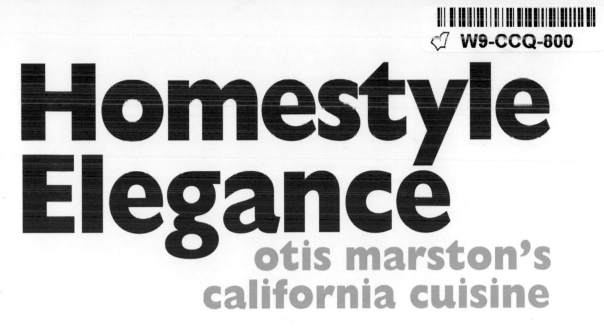

By Otis and
Sally Marston,
creators of
Marston's
Restaurant
in Pasadena

Dedicated to
our parents,
Margaret & Don Newport and
Jean & Edgar Marston, Jr.,
who gave us a love for life and people
and a desire to share that with others...
and to all married couples who work together.

Marston Products
119 East Longden Avenue
San Gabriel, CA 91775
(626) 285-1822
marstonproducts.com

ISBN 0-9716107-0-3

Cover and book design by Cheryl McLean.
Drawings by Shirley Weyand.
Cover photograph by Ju Ju.

Printed in the United States of America

Acknowledgments

Our restaurant, Marston's, in Pasadena, California, provided many amazing adventures. During the twelve years we owned Marston's, we traveled, experienced various culinary delights, and shared them with our customers and friends. We are grateful to God for providing an opportunity to serve the public and our community through our culinary creations.

This cookbook represents the energy, creativity, and love that went into the cooking in our restaurant kitchen. Many have influenced the making of this book—family members, friends, customers, restaurants, and their chefs de cuisine.

A special thank you to our daughter, Lisa, and her husband, Erich, daughter-in-law, Melinda, and our son, Otis Jr., for eating many new dishes and being flexible and patient with our busy schedule. Thank you, Otis Jr., for your many hours of assistance in running the restaurant and tireless hours of cooking alongside your dad in a very hot kitchen—sometimes reaching 130 degrees in the summer! Your support has carried us on many a weary day.

Thank you to our many friends for their prayers and support, which encouraged us year after year. A special thanks to our friend Shirley Weyand, who contributed many hours to the art work for *Homestyle Elegance*.

Thank you to Sally's sisters, Pat Newport and Donna Fraser, for their tireless hours of editing. They fueled the vision by putting feet to the book. The kitchens we've shared over the last fifty years have inspired good humor, good spirits, and good cheer. Cooking and food have brought us closer together as a family. We thank Pat's friend, and now ours, Cheryl McLean, for her creative talents in designing and publishing the book.

We trust *Homestyle Elegance* will encourage your baking, toasting, roasting, frying, boiling, stewing, sautéing, basting, braising, poaching, barbecuing, grilling, and broiling skills. May the contents please your palette, encourage your own personal creativity with food, and fill your tummy and your heart as you entertain your family and friends. The kitchen is the most amazing room in your home, offering so much pleasure! Bon Appétit!

Otis & Sally

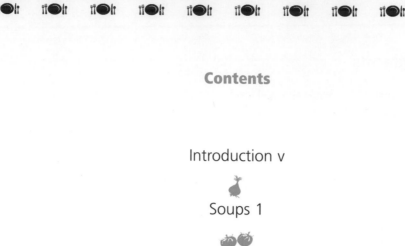

Contents

 Look for this icon to find dishes that Otis prepared when he was owner and chef of Marston's Restaurant in Pasadena.

Introduction

Homestyle Elegance…picture classic food…the freshest ingredients…simply prepared…perhaps an unexpected ingredient or surprising combination…then presented with a special garnish or sauce on the side…a memorable meal served in the warmth of your own home. Having friends in for a meal was always a pastime, for Sally's family and mine. Whether last minute or planned, extra places at the table always meant our mothers would be preparing something with an added touch. This notion of homestyle elegance became the trademark of Marston's, our Pasadena eatery that we established in 1988 and sold 12 years later. Over the years, we welcomed thousands of guests into our "home," a small bungalow with a perennially blooming garden. We served breakfast, lunch, and special dinners, offering menu items with familiar names and uncommon touches.

Cooking has been my hobby, my job, and my artistic outlet. Over the years, I've cooked thousands of recipes, created many of my own, and developed an approach to cooking that I'm eager to pass on to you. If you like to follow recipes to the letter, and many cooks do, you'll simply benefit from my tastes. But if you're willing to experiment a bit and refine your tasting technique, I encourage you to taste test your way through these recipes, varying the seasoning, substituting ingredients, and trying new presentations to create your own homestyle elegance!

A few notes about what you'll find in this book…

We're pleased to share many recipes from Marston's—you'll find those noted with this symbol. Throughout the book, I've offered some time honored tips from my kitchen to make your cooking experience more enjoyable. You'll find the tips noted in the index as well. If you wish to purchase our products, we invite you to visit our website at **marstonproducts.com**. You'll find a list of distributors for our San Pasqual Dressing, Candied Pecans, and *Homestyle Elegance*. I'll also include a recipe or tip from my latest endeavors in the kitchen. We welcome your questions, suggestions, or comments via the website.

Soups

Black Bean Andouille Soup with Crispy Tortilla Strips

A nice winter lunch option or pair this hearty soup with the Muffuletta Sandwich (page 110) for dinner.
8-10 Servings

4 tablespoons **oil**

4 tablespoons **butter**

4 cups dried **black beans**, rinsed and drained (check for stones)

2 **white onions**, chopped

2 **garlic cloves**, chopped

2 teaspoons ground **cumin**

2 teaspoons **Tabasco sauce** (more if desired)

2 tablespoons **chicken base** (find in soup section of market)

1 cup **Andouille sausage** finely chopped in food processor
    (may substitute kielbasa or other spicy sausage)

1/2 cup **cilantro**, coarsely chopped

Crispy Tortilla Strips (recipe follows)

Suggested garnishes: **sour cream,** chopped **green onion,** grated **Monterey Jack cheese, Spicy Fresh Salsa** (page 70)

▸ **Sauté** onions and garlic in soup pot.

▸ **Add** beans, cumin, Tabasco, and chicken base. **Add** about 12 cups of water, enough to cover beans by 4-6 inches.

▸ **Bring to a boil** and **add** diced sausage and cilantro. **Continue cooking** on medium heat until beans are cooked, 1-1/2-2 hours. If water boils down, **add** more and continue cooking until beans are soft.

▸ **Taste and add** more chicken base if needed.

▸ **Remove from heat** and **puree** in batches in food processor. Return to soup pot to **keep warm** and add more water if a thinner soup is desired.

▸ **Ladle** into warm soup bowls, **top** with Crispy Tortilla Strips, and **pass** garnishes.

Crispy Tortilla Strips

These crispy strips add a nice crunch on salads, chili, and black beans too!
8-10 Servings

8-10 small **corn** or **flour tortillas**

2 cups **corn** or **canola oil**

Salt (optional)

▶ **Heat** oil in cast iron or heavy large sauce pan over medium heat until hot. **Be VERY careful** when cooking with hot oil...do NOT leave oil unattended!

▶ **Cut** tortillas into strips 1/4" wide and 1" long.

▶ **Cook** in hot oil, a small handful at a time, until lightly browned.

▶ **Drain** on paper towels, **salt** lightly if desired, let **cool**, and **store** in airtight container at room temperature.

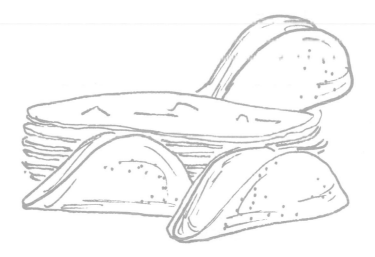

Carrot Cilantro Soup with Fresh Ginger

This is a great soup for special dinners as it is light and has a nice, tangy flavor. You may omit the ginger for a milder flavor.

6 Servings

8 cups **water**

2 pounds **carrots**, peeled and chopped

1 medium **shallot**, chopped

1/2 cup **red onion**, chopped

2 tablespoons **chicken base**

1 teaspoon freshly ground **black pepper**

1 teaspoon **Worcestershire sauce**

1/2 cup **whipping cream** or **low-fat milk**

1/2 cup **fresh cilantro**, washed and finely chopped

2 tablespoons grated **fresh ginger**

▶ In medium soup pot, **add** all ingredients except cream, cilantro, and ginger. **Cook** until carrots are soft.

▶ In food processor, **process** the carrot mixture in batches until smooth, **reserving** liquid.

▶ **Return** pureed carrot mixture to the soup pot. **Add** cream, cilantro, and fresh ginger and **heat** through.

Carrot Lentil Soup

6 Servings

2 tablespoons **butter**

2 tablespoons **canola oil**

1-1/2 cup finely chopped **carrots**

1 cup finely chopped **celery**

1 large **sweet onion**, finely chopped

2 cloves **garlic**, finely chopped

1 **shallot**, finely chopped

3 quarts **water**

2 tablespoons **beef base**

1 teaspoon **Worcestershire sauce**

1 teaspoon freshly ground **black pepper**

4 cups **lentils**, thoroughly washed

▶ In soup pot, **heat** butter and oil and **sauté** carrots, celery, onions, garlic, and shallots until soft, about 10 minutes.

▶ **Add** water to soup pot and bring to a **boil**.

▶ **Add** beef base, Worcestershire sauce and black pepper.

▶ **Add** lentils and **boil** over medium heat until soft, about 40-60 minutes.

▶ If you want a thinner soup, **add** more water and beef base to taste.

Serving suggestion: *Serve with Beer Cheese Crostini (page 75) and Fresh Pear Salad (page 33).*

Chicken Lime Vegetable Soup

This is a versatile soup...try adding other vegetables such as green beans, fresh corn or peas. For a heartier version, add rice or noodles.
8 Servings

2 tablespoons **butter**

2 tablespoons **canola oil**

3 **white onions**, chopped

5 stalks **celery**, chopped

4 **carrots**, peeled and chopped

1 cup **mushrooms**, sliced

3 quarts **water**

2 whole, **chicken breasts**, skin on (or one whole small chicken)

2 tablespoons **chicken base**

5 **Roma tomatoes**, peeled, seeded and coarsely chopped

3 tablespoons **tomato paste**

1 bunch **fresh spinach**, thoroughly washed and chopped

1 teaspoon freshly ground **black pepper**

2 tablespoons **Worcestershire sauce**

3 tablespoons **fresh lime juice**, or more to taste

1 cup **fresh parsley**, chopped

Crispy Tortilla Strips (page 3) for topping, if desired

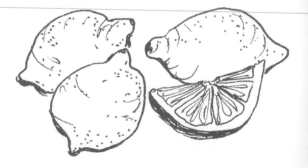

▶ **Melt** butter and oil in soup pot and **sauté** onions, celery, and carrots over medium heat for about 10 minutes. **Add** mushrooms and continue cooking about 3-5 minutes.

▶ **Add** water and chicken breasts or whole chicken and chicken base. Bring to a low **boil** and **cook** until chicken is tender, about 25 minutes for breasts and 60 minutes for a whole chicken.

▶ **Remove** chicken from pot and let **cool** until you can handle. **Reserve** liquid. Remove and **discard** skin and bones. **Dice** or **shred** chicken.

▶ **Reheat** liquid and **add** chicken, tomatoes, tomato paste, spinach, pepper, Worcestershire sauce, lime juice, and parsley.

▶ **Ladle** into warm soup bowls and **top** with Crispy Tortilla Strips (page 3).

A tip from Otis...

I like to use chicken or beef base in my soups to enhance the flavors. You can find them in the soup section of most markets. They come in jars and have a paste consistency. If you prefer not to use the prepared base, you can cook chicken or beef bones down and make a rich stock to use in place of the base and water called for in recipes.

ᵗⁱ◉ᴵⁱ Clam Chowder

This was one of the most often-requested soups at Marston's.
8-12 Servings

4 medium **russet potatoes**, peeled and diced

1/2 pound **bacon**, chopped

1 large **sweet onion,** coarsely chopped

1/2 cup **carrots**, peeled and finely chopped

1 cup **celery**, diced

1 each **red and green bell pepper**, seeded and finely chopped

4 cloves **garlic**, diced

4 cups **canned clam juice** (add another 1/2 cup if using fresh or frozen clams)

2 tablespoons **clam** or **chicken base** (clam enhances the flavor)

2 tablespoons **Worcestershire Sauce**

1 teaspoon **Tabasco sauce**

1 tablespoon freshly ground **black pepper**

3-4 cups chopped **clams,** fresh or canned (drained, but reserve juice)

1 cup **whipping cream**

10 **green onions**, chopped (optional)

▶ **Peel** and **dice** potatoes and **set aside** in cold water.

▶ **Cook** bacon in large soup pot until crisp. **Drain, reserving** 3 tablespoons of bacon grease.

▶ **Return** bacon and 3 tablespoons grease to soup pot. **Add** sweet onions, carrots, red and green bell pepper and garlic and **sauté** for 5 minutes to bring out the flavors.

▶ **Add** clam juice and, if using canned clams, **add** liquid from can.

▸ **Add** clam or chicken base and potatoes and **cook** over medium heat until the potatoes are cooked until almost tender, about 30 minutes.

▸ **Add** Worcestershire sauce, Tabasco sauce, black pepper, clams, celery and whipping cream and **simmer** over medium-low heat 15 minutes.

▸ If desired, **thicken** with cornstarch paste, adding slowly with a wire whisk.

▸ **Stir in** chopped green onion and **serve** in warm bowls.

Serving Suggestion: *For entertaining, delight your guests by serving the chowder in a bread bowl. Purchase small rounds of crusty sourdough, cut off the top, hollow out the inside, fill with chowder, replace the top, and serve immediately. Or serve with a loaf of warm crusty sour dough bread and the California Orange Salad (page 30).*

A tip from Otis...

I use cornstarch paste to thicken most of my soups and sauces. Cornstarch is a dense, powdery "flour" obtained from the endosperm of the corn kernel. It is generally mixed with a small amount of cold water to form a thin paste before adding it to a hot mixture. I use 2/3 water to 1/3 cornstarch to make my paste. To thicken soups or sauces, add small amounts of the mixture at a time to make sure you do not over thicken. Always add the paste to a hot mixture, and give it a little time to thicken.

Cream of Asparagus Soup
6 Servings

8 cups **water**

3 pounds **asparagus**, washed and ends snipped

1 **shallot**, chopped

1/2 **red onion**, chopped

2 tablespoons **chicken base**

1 teaspoon **Worcestershire Sauce**

1 teaspoon freshly ground **white** or **black pepper**

1 cup **whipping cream**

A tip from Otis...
To snip the asparagus, simply hold each spear at the ends and bend slightly. The spear naturally breaks at the point of ripeness!

▶ Bring water to a **boil** and **add** asparagus, shallot, onion, and chicken base. **Cook** over medium heat until asparagus is soft, 7-10 minutes.

▶ **Strain** soup, **reserving** all liquid.

▶ **Puree** asparagus and onions in food processor and **return** to pot. **Add** 6 cups of the asparagus broth and **cook** over medium heat.

▶ **Add** Worcestershire Sauce, pepper and whipping cream. **Thicken** with cornstarch paste if thicker consistency desired.

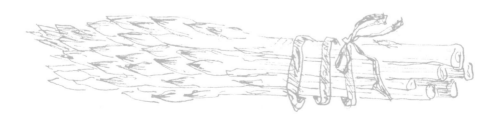

Cream of Tomato Dill Soup
8 Servings

10 medium Roma or regular **tomatoes**, peeled, seeded, cored and quartered

2 cloves **garlic**, coarsely chopped

1 teaspoon **white pepper**

1/2 **red onion**, coarsely chopped

2 tablespoons **beef base** (or more to taste)

8 cups **water**

1 cup **whipping cream** or **milk**

1 bunch **fresh dill**, finely chopped

3 tablespoons **cornstarch** mixed with 5 tablespoons **water** for thickener (optional)

Suggested garnishes: Goat Cheese Medallions (page 49), **Rye Croutons** (page 15), sprigs of **fresh dill**

> **A tip from Otis...**
> Drop whole tomatoes in boiling water for about 10 seconds and the peel will slide off in your hands!

▸ **Place** all ingredients except whipping cream and dill in a soup pot. **Boil** until onion and tomatoes are tender, about 10 minutes.

▸ **Remove** from heat and strain, **reserving** liquid in a separate bowl.

▸ **Place** remaining solids in blender and **puree** until smooth.

▸ **Return** to soup pot, **add** reserved liquid, and bring to a **boil**.

▸ Slowly **add** whipping cream and fresh dill.

▸ For a thicker soup, **add** cornstarch paste, one tablespoon at a time, **blend** with a whisk, and simmer.

▸ **Ladle** into warm soup bowls and **garnish** as desired.

Serving suggestion: *Serve with Four Cheese Macaroni (page 80) for a winter fireside dinner.*

Cream of Zucchini and Green Pea Soup

A soup that knows no season...can be served cold in summer or hot in winter.
Either way, a loaf of warm sourdough bread is the perfect accompaniment.
8 Servings

8 cups **water**

6 medium **zucchini**, sliced

1/2 medium **red onion**, chopped

3 tablespoons **chicken base**

2 **garlic** cloves, minced

1 teaspoon freshly ground **black pepper**

2 cups **frozen peas**

2 cups **whipping cream**

A tip from Otis...
I like rich soup, so you'll see whipping cream included in many of my recipes. If you want to make a lighter soup, you may substitute whole or skim milk.

▶ Bring water to a **boil** in soup pot and **add** zucchini, onion, chicken base, garlic and pepper.

▶ **Boil** until zucchini is tender, about 10-15 minutes.

▶ **Add** peas and cook 3 minutes.

▶ **Remove** from heat and **drain**, reserving all liquid. **Puree** in food processor until almost smooth.

▶ **Return** puree and liquid to pot and **stir** in cream. **Reheat** to serving temperature.

▶ **Taste** and **add** more chicken base if needed.

▶ **Ladle** into warm soup bowls and **garnish** with a few thin slices of zucchini.

Variation: *Add a touch of curry powder for a spicier soup.*

Curried Pumpkin Apple Soup

This soup is great for fall dinner parties or served with a holiday meal.
10-12 Servings

4 tablespoons **canola oil**

4 large **green apples**, cut in 16ths

2 large **sweet onions**, cut in 16ths

1 **shallot**, chopped

2 tablespoons **chicken base** (or more to taste)

1 teaspoon **curry powder** (or more to taste)

2 tablespoons **brown sugar**

1 teaspoon freshly ground **black pepper**

4 cups **half and half**

4 cups **buttermilk**

1-1/2 cans (29-ounce size) **pumpkin** (unsweetened)

3 cups **water**

Suggested garnishes: **sour cream**, roasted and salted **pepitas** (pumpkin seeds)

▸ **Heat** canola oil in large soup pot and **sauté** apples, onions, and shallot over medium heat until soft, about 15 minutes.

▸ **Puree** in food processor and **return** to pot.

▸ **Add** chicken base, curry powder, brown sugar, black pepper, half and half, pumpkin, and water. **Cook** over medium **heat** for 30 minutes stirring continually. **Add** buttermilk.

▸ **Thicken** with cornstarch paste if necessary.

▸ **Garnish** with sour cream and **sprinkle** roasted and salted pepitas on top.

French Onion Soup with Otis's Fresh Baked Rye Croutons

6-8 Servings

2 tablespoons **olive oil** or **canola oil**

4 large **sweet onions** (Maui, Walla Walla, or white), slice in half, then in 1/4-inch slices

1 tablespoon **sugar**

8 cups **water**

2 tablespoons **beef base**

1 tablespoon **Worcestershire sauce**

1 teaspoon freshly ground **black pepper**

1 tablespoon **sherry**

1 cup grated **Fontina cheese**

Otis's Fresh Baked Croutons (recipe follows)

▸ **Heat** oil in large soup pot and **add** onions, sugar and 1/2 cup of water. **Sauté** for 45 minutes over medium-low heat, **stirring** often, until brown in color.

▸ **Add** remaining water, beef base, Worcestershire sauce, pepper and sherry and **cook** another 30 minutes.

▸ **Ladle** into bowls and **top** with grated cheese and croutons. Place bowls on a tray and place under **broiler** until cheese melts. (I like a lot of cheese!)

Otis's Fresh Baked Rye Croutons

6 slices **rye bread**, cut in 1/4- to 1/2-inch cubes with crust on (may use French or sourdough bread)

4 tablespoons **Parmesan cheese**

4 tablespoons **butter**

1 teaspoon **Montreal Seasoning** (or seasoned salt)

▸ **Preheat** oven to 325 degrees.

▸ **Place** diced bread on cookie sheet and **drizzle** melted butter over bread.

▸ **Mix** Parmesan cheese and Montreal Seasoning or seasoned salt and **sprinkle** it over the cubes of bread. **Toss** well to coat all pieces.

▸ **Bake** until crisp and firm, about 30 minutes, **stirring** every 10 minutes.

▸ **Serve** warm or cool and **store** in airtight container.

Meatless Minestrone
10-12 Servings

2 tablespoons **butter**

2 tablespoons **canola oil**

1 large **onion**, chopped

5 cloves **garlic**, finely chopped

1 cup **celery**, chopped

1 large **carrot**, sliced

1 **shallot** , finely chopped

1 15-1/2 ounce can **garbanzo beans** with juice

1 15-1/2 ounce can **kidney beans** with juice

1 15-1/2 ounce can **Great Northern beans**, drained

1 11 ounce can of **white shoepeg** (or yellow) **corn**

1 28 ounce can of Italian recipe peeled **tomatoes**

8 cups **water**

1-1/2 teaspoons freshly ground **black pepper**

1 teaspoon **Worcestershire sauce**

2 **bay leaves**

3 tablespoons **chicken base** (or 2 tablespoons chicken base and 1 tablespoon beef base)

3 tablespoons **tomato paste**

2 **zucchini**, diced

2 **yellow squash**, diced

1/2 head **Napa** (or regular green) **cabbage**, sliced

2-3 cups **penne pasta**, cooked al dente and set aside

1 bunch of **Italian parsley**, coarsely chopped

3 cups **fresh spinach** leaves, chopped

2 cups freshly grated **Parmesan cheese**

- In large soup pot heat butter and oil and **sauté** onion, garlic, celery, carrot, and shallot until tender, about 5 minutes.

- **Add** garbanzo, kidney and Great Northern beans, corn, tomatoes, and water.

- **Add** pepper, Worcestershire sauce, bay leaves, chicken base, and tomato paste.

- **Cook** over medium heat for 30 minutes.

- **Add** zucchini, squash, and cabbage, and **cook** another 20 minutes.

- **Add** pasta, Italian parsley, and spinach, and **continue cooking** another 10 minutes.

- **Serve** with freshly grated Parmesan cheese.

Note: *When reheating the minestrone, you may need to add some more water. When you do, also add more chicken base, to taste.*

Otis's Corn Chowder

Another Martson's Restaurant favorite!
6-8 Servings

3 tablespoons **bacon grease** or canola oil

1 **red onion**, coarsely chopped

3 cloves **garlic**, minced

2 **Andouille sausages** and/or 4 slices of **bacon**, diced and cooked

2 cups **water**

2 13-ounce cans of **whole kernel corn** with juice

2 tablespoons **chicken base**

1 teaspoon **Tabasco sauce**

1 teaspoon **Worcestershire sauce**

1 teaspoon freshly ground **black pepper**

1 each **red and green bell peppers**, seeded and diced

2 cups **whipping cream** or milk

6 **green onions**, chopped (use both tops and greens)

▸ **Heat** bacon grease or oil in soup pot and **sauté** onion and garlic over medium heat for 5 minutes. **Add** sausage and/or cooked bacon.

▸ **Add** water, corn with juice, chicken base, Tabasco sauce, Worcestershire sauce, pepper, and red and green bell peppers and **boil** slowly for 30 minutes.

▸ **Add** whipping cream and green onion and **heat** to serving temperature, **stirring** frequently. **Thicken** with cornstarch paste, if desired.

▸ **Ladle** into warm mugs.

Variations: *Fold in portions of bay shrimp or grilled chopped chicken breast for a hearty meal. You may also add a cup or two of cooked black beans*

Potato Leek Cheese Soup
8-10 Servings

3/4 pound **bacon**, chopped

2 large **leeks**, coarsely chopped **white ends only**

1 **white onion**, finely chopped

1 **shallot**, finely diced

2 cloves **garlic**, minced

10 cups **water**

5 large **russet potatoes**, peeled, diced, and reserved in cold water

2 tablespoons **chicken base**

2 cups **whipping cream** (or milk if a thinner consistency is desired)

1 tablespoon **Worcestershire sauce**

2 cups **Fontina cheese**, grated

2 cups cheddar or **Swiss cheese**, grated

1 teaspoon freshly ground **black pepper**

Suggested garnishes: **Croutons** (page 15), crisp **bacon bits**

▸ In large soup pot, **cook** bacon until crisp. **Remove** and **drain**. **Reserve** 2 tablespoons of grease.

▸ **Add** reserved bacon grease, leeks, onion, shallot, and garlic and **sauté** over medium heat for 10 minutes.

▸ **Add** water, potatoes (drained), and chicken base, and **boil** until potatoes are soft, about 20-30 minutes.

▸ **Mash** potatoes with wire whisk in pot with liquid. **Add** whipping cream and Worcestershire sauce and all but 1/3 cup bacon. **Heat** over medium heat.

▸ **Add** grated cheeses and **continue cooking** over medium-low heat, **stirring** with a wire whisk, until cheese is melted. **Watch** closely so it does not burn!

▸ **Ladle** into warm soup bowls. **Garnish** with croutons and chopped cooked bacon.

Roasted Red Bell Pepper Soup

This is a wonderful addition to a special dinner party menu — light and elegant!
4-6 Servings

8 large **red bell peppers**

4 cups **water**

2 **garlic** cloves, finely chopped

1 tablespoon **Worcestershire sauce**

1/2 **red onion**, chopped

1 **shallot**, finely chopped

2 tablespoons **chicken base**

1 teaspoon **white pepper**

1 cup **whipping cream** or milk

Cornstarch paste

▶ **Roast** red peppers over open flame on gas stove, **turning** frequently with tongs. When soft and black, **peel, seed**, and coarsely **chop** peppers. **Save** juice from bag and **add** it to the soup (see tip).

▶ **Combine** peppers and all ingredients except whipping cream in a soup pot. **Boil** slowly for 20 minutes.

▶ **Remove** from heat and **puree** mixture in a food processor.

▶ **Return** to soup pot, **add** whipping cream and **reheat** for about 10 minutes, **stirring** frequently. **Thicken** with cornstarch paste, if desired.

A tip from Otis...

I like to roast peppers over the gas on my cooktop. I put them directly over the flame and turn them frequently with tongs until they are blackened. Then I put them in a plastic bag for about an hour...this makes them easy to peel. You can also roast them on the barbecue, which adds a nice flavor!

Split Pea Soup with Ham and Andouille Sausage

8-10 Servings

1/2 pound **bacon**, chopped

2 **white onions**, finely chopped

4 stalks **celery**, finely chopped

1 cup **carrots**, peeled and finely chopped

3 **garlic** cloves, finely chopped

1 tablespoon **Worcestershire sauce**

1 teaspoon freshly ground **black pepper**

2 tablespoons **chicken base**

4 cups **dried split peas**

2-3 **smoked ham hocks** (approximately 1-1/4 pounds)

1/4 pound **Andouille sausage**, cooked and diced (can use ham or smoked pork)

12 cups **water**

▶ **Cook** bacon in large soup pot until crisp. **Drain, reserving** 3 tablespoons of bacon grease in pot. **Add** onions, celery, carrots, and garlic and **sauté** for 5 minutes.

▶ **Add** Worcestershire sauce, pepper and chicken base.

▶ **Add** split peas, ham hocks, sausage, and water, and **boil** slowly for 2 hours. **Check** the pot every 15 minutes and **stir**. If water is boiling off too rapidly, **add** more.

▶ **Remove** ham hocks from pot, **cut** all meat off bone and **return** meat to pot. If soup is too thick, **add** more water and chicken base to taste.

Summary White Gazpacho

This was a menu favorite when we owned Marston's...a great lunch for those "too hot to eat" days. We served it with a basket of our Cheddar Cheese Popovers (page 78).
8-10 Servings

4 **cucumbers**, peeled, seeded, and finely chopped (hot house are best)

2 small or one large **red onion**, finely chopped

3 cups cold **water**

1 pint low-fat **plain yogurt** (more for thicker consistency)

2 tablespoons **chicken base**

1 teaspoon **Tabasco sauce**

1 teaspoon **Worcestershire sauce**

2 ripe **avocados**, finely chopped

2 large **tomatoes**, peeled, cored, and finely chopped

1 teaspoon freshly ground **black pepper**

6 **green onions**, chopped

Suggested garnishes: **sour cream**, **fresh chives,** and **lime** slices

▸ **Puree** half of the chopped cucumber and half of the chopped red onion in a food processor.

▸ **Combine** water, yogurt, chicken base, pepper, Tabasco sauce, and Worcestershire sauce in a large pot.

▸ **Add** both chopped and pureed cucumber and onion. **Stir** in avocados, tomatoes, and pepper.

▸ **Add** green onions and more yogurt if desired, but be careful — too much yogurt will make the gazpacho taste chalky. **Taste** and add more chicken base if desired.

▸ **Refrigerate** for 2-3 hours until well chilled.

▸ **Garnish** with dollop of sour cream, fresh chives, and thinly sliced lime.

Variations: *Add one cup of Caramelized Onions (page 59).*

White Bean and Chicken Cilantro Sausage Soup

8 Servings

4 tablespoons **canola oil**

1-1/2 cups **carrots**, chopped

1-1/2 cups **celery**, chopped

4 cups **small white** or **Great Northern beans** (dried)

1 large **white onion**, chopped

2 cloves **garlic**, minced

1 **shallot**, diced

2 tablespoons **chicken base**

4 quarts **water** (or combination of chicken stock and water)

4 tablespoons **tomato paste**

1-1/2 pounds **chicken cilantro sausage**, diced and cooked (may use kielbasa)

▸ **Heat** oil in soup pot and **sauté** carrots and celery until lightly cooked.

▸ **Add** beans, onion, garlic, shallot, chicken base, and water.

▸ **Cook** about 1 hour, until beans are tender.

▸ **Add** tomato paste and sausage and **continue cooking** 15 minutes. If too thick, add water. Always **check** flavor when you add more water — you may need more chicken base.

▸ **Ladle** into warm soup bowls.

Yukon Gold Potato and Leek Soup with Crab

8-10 Servings

1/2 pound **bacon**, chopped

3 large **leeks**, white ends only, finely chopped

2 cloves **garlic**, minced

1 **carrot**, peeled and finely chopped

1 large **white onion**, chopped

5 large **Yukon Gold potatoes**, peeled, diced, and reserved in cold water

10 cups **water**

2 tablespoons **chicken base**

1 cup **whipping cream** or milk

1 teaspoon ground **black pepper**

1 pound **fresh crab meat**

▸ **Cook** bacon in soup pot until crisp. **Drain**, **reserving** 2 tablespoons of bacon grease in pot. **Add** leeks, garlic, carrot, and onion and **sauté** for 10 minutes.

▸ **Drain** the potatoes and **add** to soup pot along with chicken base and water.

▸ **Boil** until potatoes are tender, about 30 minutes. **Remove** from heat and **mash** with wire whisk.

▸ **Add** whipping cream and pepper.

▸ **Ladle** into warm soup bowls and **garnish** with fresh crab meat.

Serving suggestion: *Serve with California Orange Salad (page 30), omitting chicken.*

Variation: *In place of crab meat, garnish with black mussels and clams, fresh corn cut off the cob, or diced green onions. Steam mussels and clams in clam juice and be sure to discard those that don't open!*

Zucchini Thai Curry Soup
6 Servings

5 medium **zucchini**, peeled and chopped

2 cloves **garlic**, finely chopped

1/2 small **red onion**, finely chopped

3 quarts **water**

2 tablespoons **chicken base**

2 teaspoons **turmeric**

2-3 tablespoons **curry powder** (depending on your taste!)

2 teaspoons **Hoisin sauce** (found in Chinese food section of market)

1 cup **whipping cream**

Suggested garnishes: **Hoisin sauce,** chopped **green onions**

▶ **Combine** zucchini, garlic, onion, and water in soup pot. **Cook** until soft, about 20 minutes.

▶ **Puree** mixture in food processor and **return** to pot.

▶ **Add** chicken base, turmeric, curry powder, Hoisin Sauce, and whipping cream and **cook** over medium heat for 30 minutes.

▶ **Adjust** flavoring to taste and **thicken** with cornstarch paste if desired.

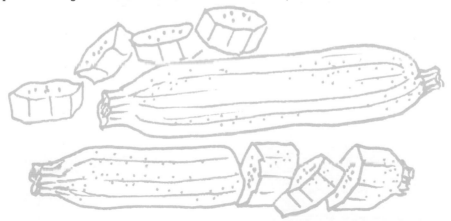

Salads

Arugula Salad with Balsamic Mustard Vinaigrette

This makes a great main course when topped with grilled salmon, chicken breast or bay shrimp.
4-6 Servings

3 bunches crisp **arugula**, washed, drained, and torn

1/2 cup **Feta cheese**, crumbled

1/4 cup **pine nuts** or **chopped hazelnuts**, toasted

12 **fresh asparagus** spears, blanched and diagonally sliced

1 **red bell pepper**, seeded, thinly sliced

▸ **Toss** all ingredients in chilled salad bowl with Balsamic Mustard Vinaigrette.

Note: *When toasting pine nuts, be careful not to overheat—they get dark very easily.*

Balsamic Mustard Vinaigrette

1 cup **olive oil**

2 tablespoons **Dijon-style mustard**

6 tablespoons **balsamic vinegar**

2 tablespoons **rice vinegar**

4 **garlic** cloves, minced

Salt and freshly ground **black pepper** to taste

▸ **Mix** all ingredients in blender and **serve** at room temperature.

Butter Lettuce Salad with Lime Dijon Dressing

6 Servings

2 heads **butter lettuce**, washed, dried and chilled

1 large **Granny Smith apple**, julienned

1 large **avocado**, chopped

1/2 cup salted **pistachio nuts**, chopped

▶ **Tear** lettuce leaves and **toss** with apples, avocado and nuts. **Pour** dressing over salad, **toss** and serve.

Lime Dijon Dressing

1 **egg**, coddled

2 teaspoons fresh **Parmesan cheese**, grated

1/2 teaspoon **salt**

1/2 teaspoon freshly ground **black pepper**

2 tablespoons **Dijon-style mustard**

2 tablespoons **fresh lime juice**

1 teaspoon **Worcestershire sauce**

1 teaspoon **sugar**

1/2 cup **vegetable oil**

▶ **Combine** all dressing ingredients in a blender and **blend** for 2 or 3 minutes. **Refrigerate** for at least one hour. **Mix** well before serving.

California Orange Salad

This was always the most popular luncheon menu selection at our restaurant! For a side salad at dinner, simply omit the chicken.

8 Servings

2 heads **iceberg lettuce**, rinsed and chopped

1 head **red leaf lettuce**, washed, dried, and chopped (or use all romaine, if desired)

2 **avocados**, peeled and chopped

1 cup **Marston's Candied Pecans** (page 64)

1/2 cup **black raisins**

2 large **green apples**, unpeeled and finely chopped (tart ones like Granny Smith are best)

4 **green onions**, finely chopped heads and tops

2 cups **mandarin oranges**, drained, or 3 **oranges**, peeled, sectioned, and chopped

1/2 cup crumbled **blue cheese**

1 cup **Marston's San Pasqual Dressing** (see note)

1/2 cup **chicken breast** per person, boned, skinned, cooked, and chopped

▸ **Mix** all ingredients in chilled salad bowl and serve on chilled plates.

Serving suggestions: *Serve with a basket of warm Cheddar Cheese Popovers (page 78).*

NOTE: *If using fresh oranges, be sure they're not bitter. For a list of distributors of Marston's San Pasqual Dressing and Candied Pecans, go to* **marstonproducts.com**.

Cordierra Salad with Grilled Chicken

Named after the Cordierra Resort in the Rocky Mountains, a favorite hiking and fishing destination for the Marston family.
4-6 Servings

2 heads **Romaine lettuce**, washed, dried, and torn

4 **Roma tomatoes**, cored and chopped

2 **avocados**, peeled and diced (hold out slices for garnish)

12 each **large black** and **green olives**, sliced

6 slices of **bacon**, chopped, cooked and drained

3/4 cup crumbled **blue cheese**

3/4 cup **Marston's Candied Pecans** (page 64)

1 cup **Marston's San Pasqual Salad Dressing** (see Note)

Grilled Chicken

4 **chicken breasts**, boned, skinned and grilled

1 tablespoon **Montreal seasoning** (or seasoned salt)

1 tablespoon **flour**

2 teaspoons **sesame seeds**

2 tablespoons **butter**

2 tablespoons **vegetable oil**

▸ **Toss** all salad ingredients and dressing together in a chilled bowl. **Divide** portions among chilled salad plates, **top** with grilled, diagonally sliced chicken breast and **garnish** with a slice of avocado.

▸ Our favorite way to grill chicken for salads is to **coat** breasts with a mixture of Montreal Seasoning, flour, and sesame seeds and **sauté** them in butter and oil until nicely browned on each side and cooked all the way through, about 15 minutes. They'll keep in the refrigerator for two days.

NOTE: *For a list of distributors of Marston's San Pasqual Dressing and Candied Pecans, go to* **marstonproducts.com**.

Fresh Fig and Gorgonzola Salad
4 Servings

1/2 cup **Gorgonzola cheese**, crumbled

1/2 cup **roasted walnuts**, chopped

8 cups **gourmet salad greens**

8 **fresh figs**, quartered

Vinaigrette

▶ **Toss** cheese, nuts, greens, and dressing together.

▶ **Place** on chilled salad plates and arrange figs on top.

Variations: *If fresh figs aren't available, you may substitute dried figs or fresh mangoes or papayas for an equally elegant salad! For a more complex flavor, add 1/2 cup of pancetta bacon, diced and cooked until crisp.*

Vinaigrette

1/3 cup **balsamic vinegar**

3/4 cup **extra virgin olive oil**

1 teaspoon **lemon juice**

Salt and freshly ground **black pepper** to taste

▶ **Mix** all ingredients together in blender.

▶ For a fruitier flavor, you can **add** 3 peeled and seeded fresh figs before blending.

Fresh Pear Salad
4 Servings

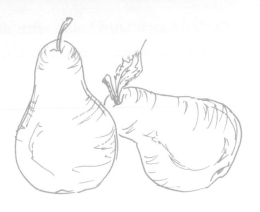

8 cups **gourmet salad greens**
1/2 cup **Marston's San Pasqual Dressing** (see Note)
2 ripe **Bartlett pears**, thinly sliced, skin on
2 **avocados**, peeled and diced
12 ounces **Roquefort** or **goat cheese**, crumbled
1/2 cup **Marston's Candied Pecans**, chopped (page 64)
Fresh blackberries or **raspberries** (optional)

▸ **Combine** salad greens with dressing and place in center of chilled individual plates.

▸ **Lay** pear slices around edge of plates.

▸ **Sprinkle** cheese, avocado, and candied pecans over salad.

▸ **Drizzle** a little more dressing over each salad.

▸ **Garnish**, if desired, with fresh berries..

▸ **Or**…you can simply **toss** all ingredients together!

NOTE: *For a list of distributors of Marston's San Pasqual Dressing and Candied Pecans, go to* **marstonproducts.com**.

Grilled Lamb Loin Salad with Rosemary Balsamic Vinaigrette

A tasty dinner entrée...serve with crusty bread! The lamb is best when marinated overnight.
4 Servings

1 to 1-1/2 pounds **lamb tenderloin**, trimmed

1/2 cup **olive oil**

2 **garlic** cloves, minced

6 small **red potatoes**, quartered

2 tablespoons **butter**

1/4 cup **Parmesan cheese**

3/4 cup **Feta cheese**, crumbled

1/2 cup **red onion**, diced

4 medium **Roma tomatoes**, diced

1 teaspoon **fresh rosemary**, minced

1/2 cup **artichoke hearts**, quartered

4 cups **gourmet salad greens**

1/2 cup **Rosemary Balsamic Vinaigrette** (recipe follows)

LAMB

▸ **Mix** olive oil and garlic, **pour** over lamb and **marinate** overnight in refrigerator.

▸ **Preheat** oven to 375 degrees.

▸ **Brown** in frying pan and place, uncovered, in oven. **Cook** for 10 minutes or more for desired doneness. Most people like it medium rare. *(Do not start lamb until potatoes are cooked.)*

▸ **Slice** thinly and set aside. **Keep warm** for serving.

POTATOES

▸ **Toss** potatoes, butter and Parmesan cheese together and place in baking pan.

▸ **Bake** uncovered at 400 degrees for approximately 40 minutes, turning once, until crispy.

SALAD

▸ **Toss** Feta cheese, onion, tomatoes, rosemary, artichoke hearts, potatoes, lettuce, and vinaigrette together. **Place** on chilled plates and **arrange** thin slices of lamb on top.

Rosemary Balsamic Vinaigrette

1 cup **olive oil**

2 tablespoons **Dijon-style mustard**

6 tablespoons **balsamic vinegar**

2 tablespoons **rice vinegar**

1 teaspoon **lemon juice**

1 teaspoon **fresh rosemary**, finely chopped

4 **garlic** cloves, minced

1/4 cup **mayonnaise**

Salt and freshly ground **black pepper** to taste

▸ **Mix** all ingredients together with wire whisk and store in refrigerator.

Jicama Salad

We served this at Marston's with Crab Cappellini and Honey Mustard Sauce (page 98). It's also a perfect salad to serve with Mexican food!

4 Servings

2 large **jicama**, peeled, cut in matchstick pieces
1/2 **red bell pepper**, julienned
1/2 **yellow bell pepper**, julienned
1 medium **red onion**, thinly sliced
1/3 cup **fresh orange juice**
2 tablespoons **rice vinegar**
Salt and freshly ground **black pepper** to taste

▶ **Combine** jicama, red and yellow bell pepper, and onion in bowl.

▶ **Mix** orange juice, vinegar, salt and pepper together and **pour** over salad mixture.

▶ **Refrigerate** for at least one hour (overnight is better) and **serve** well chilled.

Variation: *To spice up the flavor, add a few red chili flakes to the dressing.*

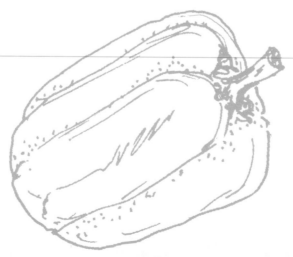

Jicama and Pineapple Salad with Cilantro Vinaigrette
4-6 Servings

1 package fresh **baby spinach**
1 small **jicama**, peeled and cut into 3" long matchstick pieces
1 cup fresh **pineapple**, cubed
1/2 cup **pine nuts**, toasted
1/2 cup **cilantro** leaves
Cilantro Vinaigrette Dressing (recipe follows)

▶ **Toss** spinach, jicama, pineapple, pine nuts and cilantro leaves in a large bowl.

▶ **Add** enough dressing to coat and **divide** among chilled salad plates.

Cilantro Vinaigrette

1/3 cup **vegetable oil**
3 tablespoons **white wine vinegar**
1 tablespoon **shallot**, minced
1/4 cup **cilantro**, chopped
1/4 teaspoon **cumin**
Salt and freshly ground **black pepper** to taste

▶ **Whisk** oil, vinegar, shallot, cilantro and cumin in a small bowl to blend.

Lobster and Avocado Salad with Green Goddess Dressing
4 Servings

4 cups of **gourmet salad greens**
1/2 head **iceberg lettuce**, thinly sliced
1/2 cup (or to taste) **Green Goddess Dressing** (recipe follows)
2 **avocados**, peeled and thinly sliced
4 **lobster tails**, boiled, chilled and thinly sliced (jumbo shrimp may be substituted)
4 **hard-boiled eggs**, sliced
2 medium **tomatoes**, peeled, cored, and cut into wedges
12 **fresh asparagus spears**, blanched, chilled, and diagonally sliced

▸ **Mix** lettuce and **divide** among chilled salad plates.

▸ **Arrange** half a sliced avocado on top of lettuce.

▸ **Place** sliced lobster tail on top of avocado.

▸ **Pour** chilled dressing over salad. **Garnish** with eggs, tomatoes, and asparagus.

Green Goddess Dressing

2 **lemons**, juiced

2 teaspoons prepared **Dijon-style mustard**

3 cloves **garlic**, minced

2 tablespoons **tarragon vinegar**

1/2 teaspoon **salt**

1 teaspoon **white pepper**

1 tablespoon **Maggi seasoning** (found in the spice section of most markets)

1/2 bunch **fresh parsley**, finely chopped

1/4 cup **fresh chives**, finely chopped

1 ounce **anchovy paste**

1 cup **mayonnaise**

1 cup **sour cream**

▸ **Place** all ingredients except mayonnaise and sour cream in large bowl of electric mixer. **Mix** on medium speed for about a minute to blend ingredients.

▸ **Add** mayonnaise and sour cream and **blend** on medium speed for 5 minutes until well blended.

▸ **Store** in refrigerator for up to a week.

Mesclun Salad with Goat Cheese, Mangoes and Dried Cranberries

4 Servings

6 cups **mesclun** lettuce, washed, dried, chilled, and torn

1/2 cup **goat cheese**, crumbled

1/2 cup **pine nuts**, toasted

1/2 cup **dried cranberries**

1 **mango**, peeled and diced

Lime Dijon Dressing (page 29)

▶ **Toss** all ingredients, **drizzle** with chilled Lime Dijon Dressing and **serve** on cold plates.

A tip from Otis...

Mesclun is the French Provençal term given to a mixture of tender young lettuce and greens. While the ingredients in mesclun are traditionally varied, its hallmark is a wonderful combination of colors, textures and flavors. Radicchio may be added for more contrast. You may make your own combination of mesclun or buy it already prepared in the market.

Oriental Chicken Salad

6-8 Servings

3 whole **chicken breasts** (6 halves)
24-32 small **won ton wrappers** (4 per person)
4 cups **canola oil**
1 head **red leaf lettuce**, washed, dried, and chopped
2 heads **iceberg lettuce**, washed, thinly sliced, and chilled
6 **green onions**, whites and tops, thinly sliced
2 cups **mandarin oranges**, drained and chilled
1/3 cup **sesame seeds**, toasted
1/3 cup **mixed nuts**, chopped
1 cup bottled **soy ginger dressing**

▶ **Preheat** oven to 375 degrees.

▶ **Wrap** chicken breasts in foil and **bake** for about 30 minutes. **Cool** and **shred** or dice.

▶ **Heat** oil in frying pan and brown won ton wrappers. **Drain** on paper towels. Allow to **cool** then **break** them up to use in salad.

▶ **Toss** all ingredients in a large bowl, **reserving** a handful of crushed won ton wrappers for a garnish and half of the sesame seeds for the top of each salad.

Otis's Caesar Salad

Topped with Blackened Salmon (facing page), this becomes a sumptuous entrée.
4-6 Servings

2 heads **romaine lettuce** (hearts only)

3 **Roma tomatoes**, cored and quartered

1 **avocado**, peeled and diced

3/4 cup freshly grated **Parmesan cheese** (use the very best you can find!)

1 cup **Croutons** (page 15)

1/4 cup **Caesar Dressing**

▸ Thoroughly **wash** lettuce and **wrap** in paper towels to dry. **Chill** in refrigerator.

▸ **Tear** lettuce and **toss** with avocado, croutons, and dressing.

▸ **Add** tomatoes and Parmesan cheese. **Toss** again.

Caesar Dressing

1 **coddled egg** (cook egg in shell in boiling water for about 90 seconds)

2 cloves **garlic**, minced

1/8 teaspoon **Worcestershire sauce**

1/8 teaspoon **Tabasco sauce**

1-1/2 cups **olive oil**

1/2 teaspoon freshly ground **black pepper**

1/2 **lemon**, juiced

1 teaspoon **Dijon-style mustard** (or more to taste)

3 tablespoons **red wine vinegar**

1 2-ounce can **anchovies**

▸ **Mix** all ingredients in blender until smooth.

Variation: *For a spicier dressing, add 1-2 jalapeno peppers, seeded and finely chopped.*

Otis's Blackened Salmon Caesar Salad

4-6 serving size **fillets of salmon**, skinned
2 teaspoons **Cajun spice**
1 teaspoon each **salt** and freshly ground **black pepper**
2 tablespoons **butter**
2 tablespoons **olive oil**

▸ **Mix** Cajun spice, salt, and pepper and **coat** both sides of each piece of salmon.

▸ **Melt** butter and oil in frying pan and **grill** salmon on both sides until dark brown.

▸ **Simmer** until done, 7 to 10 minutes depending on thickness.

▸ **Lay** salmon fillet on top of dressed Caesar Salad (facing page).

A tip from Otis...
To chill lettuce...
▸ For any lettuce except iceberg, submerge the head of lettuce in water, shake, and drain core side down. Submerge again and cut the end off and drain, standing up in a dish in the refrigerator. Cover with plastic wrap or in a plastic bag and place in refrigerator. Lettuce will stay fresh for up to 7 days.
▸ For iceberg lettuce, core and submerge the head in water, then shake and drain, core side down, in a covered container in the refrigerator.

Otis's Cobb Salad

4-6 Servings

2 heads **iceberg lettuce**, finely chopped

4 **Roma tomatoes**, cored and chopped

2 **avocados**, peeled and diced

8 slices **bacon**, chopped, cooked and drained

3/4 cup **blue cheese**, crumbled

4 **hard-boiled eggs**

2 cups **chicken breast**, cooked and diced

1 cup bottled **Italian dressing** (Wishbone dressing is best)

1/2 to 1 cup of **Otis's Blue Cheese Dressing**

▸ **Toss** all ingredients. **Serve** on chilled plates.

Otis's Blue Cheese Dressing

2 cups **buttermilk**

1 cup **sour cream**

1 cup **mayonnaise**

2 **garlic** cloves, minced

1 teaspoon freshly ground **black pepper**

1 teaspoon **red wine vinegar**

1-1/2 ounces **Hidden Valley Buttermilk Ranch Dressing** mix (dry)

1 cup **blue cheese**, crumbled

▸ **Place** all ingredients except blue cheese in bowl and **mix** well.

▸ **Fold** in blue cheese.

▸ **Refrigerate** for at least 2 hours before serving. Will keep refrigerated for about a week.

Cobb Salad Variation
4-6 Servings

2 heads **romaine lettuce**, finely chopped

1 cup button **mushrooms**, finely chopped

2 large **Roma tomatoes**, finely chopped

1/2 cup **bacon**, chopped, cooked and drained

1/2 cup **black olives**, sliced

2 ripe **avocados**, diced

6 ounces **blue cheese**, crumbled

1/2 cup **Marston's San Pasqual Dressing** (or more to taste)

▶ **Toss** all ingredients in chilled salad bowl and serve.

NOTE: *For a list of distributors of Marston's San Pasqual Dressing and other products, go to* **marstonproducts.com**.

Pasadena Salad

*The Little Old Ladies from Pasadena **love** this salad! We always served this with Cheddar Cheese Popovers (page 78).*
4 Servings

8 cups **spinach**, washed and dried

1/2 pound **bacon**, chopped, cooked, and drained

4 **green onions**, whites and tops, thinly sliced

1 **avocado**, diced

1/3 cup **Marston's Candied Pecans** (page 64)

2 whole **chicken breasts** (4 halves)

1/2 cup **Marston's San Pasqual Dressing** (or more to taste)

▸ **Preheat** oven to 375 degrees.

▸ **Wrap** chicken breasts in foil and **bake** for 30-40 minutes.
   Cool and **shred**.

▸ **Toss** all ingredients in large bowl and **divide** among chilled salad plates.

NOTE: *For a list of distributors of Marston's San Pasqual Dressing and Candied Pecans, go to* **marstonproducts.com**.

Romaine and Bay Shrimp Salad with Blue Cheese Dressing

4 Servings

1 head **romaine lettuce**, washed and cut in quarters lengthwise

16 ounces **bay shrimp**

2 **Roma tomatoes**, finely chopped

1/2 cup fresh or frozen **peas** (optional)

Croutons made with Kalamata olive bread (page 15)

▸ **Place** a portion of romaine lettuce on each chilled plate.

▸ **Top** with shrimp, tomatoes, and peas.

▸ **Drizzle** dressing over salad and **garnish** with croutons.

Blue Cheese Dressing Variation

1 cup imported **blue cheese**, crumbled

1 cup **sour cream**

1 cup **mayonnaise**

4 ounces **Hidden Valley Buttermilk Ranch Dressing** mix (dry)

1 teaspoon **Worcestershire sauce**

1 cup **vegetable oil**

1 teaspoon freshly ground **black pepper**

1 teaspoon **red wine vinegar**

3 cloves **garlic**, minced

4 tablespoons fresh **parsley**, chopped

▸ **Blend** all ingredients with a wire whisk.

Sautéed Shrimp Salad with Goat Cheese Medallions

This is a nice salad as a dinner entrée served with olive bread.
4-6 Servings

24 **gulf shrimp**, peeled and deveined

16 **shallot cloves**, roasted

3 tablespoons **olive oil**

3 cloves **garlic**, minced

4 tablespoons **real maple syrup**

1 **red bell pepper**, julienned

1/2 cup **Marston's Candied Pecans** (page 64)

2 **avocados**, peeled and diced

4 cups **gourmet salad greens**

1 **mango**, peeled and diced

Goat Cheese Medallions (recipe follows)

1/2 cup **Sautéed Shrimp Salad Dressing** (recipe follows)

▶ **Clean** and devein shrimp. **Set aside** in refrigerator.

▶ **Peel** shallots and **wrap** in foil. **Bake** for 45 minutes. **Remove** from oven, open foil, and let cool.

▶ **Prepare** 8 goat cheese medallions.

▶ **Sauté** shrimp in olive oil with garlic just until done. **Pour** off any excess oil. **Add** maple syrup, red bell pepper strips, and pecans. **Sauté** for 2 or 3 minutes more. **Set aside** and **keep warm**.

▶ **Combine** avocados and salad greens. **Toss** with dressing. **Divide** among chilled salad plates.

▶ **Top** with goat cheese medallions, roasted shallots, mango, and shrimp mixture.

Goat Cheese Medallions

3/4 cup **Panko bread crumbs** (found in Asian foods section of your market or use plain bread crumbs)

1/4 teaspoon **seasoned salt** or Montreal Seasoning

8 ounce log of **goat cheese**

1 **egg**, lightly beaten

2 tablespoons **butter**

2 tablespoons **olive oil**

> **A tip from Otis...**
> To make clean cuts of goat cheese without flattening the log, cut with a piece of thread or unflavored dental floss. Just slide the thread under the log, cross the ends, and pull through.

▸ **Mix** bread crumbs and seasoned salt or Montreal Seasoning in small bowl.

▸ **Cut** goat cheese into 8 rounds. **Dredge** each in egg, then **coat** in bread crumbs on both sides.

▸ **Heat** butter and olive oil in frying pan and lightly **brown** medallions. **Remove** from pan and drain on paper towels.

▸ If not serving right away, **reheat** in 375 degree oven for 10 minutes.

Sautéed Shrimp Salad Dressing

1/2 cup **olive oil**

1/2 cup **mayonnaise**

2 tablespoons **balsamic vinegar**

1 tablespoon **rice vinegar**

1 **garlic** clove, minced

1/4 teaspoon **red chili flakes**

1 teaspoon freshly ground **black pepper**

▸ **Whisk** all ingredients together and **refrigerate**.

Soft Shell Crab Salad

This is an elegant and easy-to-prepare salad for a dinner party.
2 Servings

2 **soft shell crabs**, fried (or use grilled ahi steaks)

4 cups **gourmet salad greens**

3/4 cup **fresh peas**, blanched

1 **red bell pepper**, seeded and diced

1/4 cup **chives**, chopped

1 **shallot**, finely chopped

2/3 cup **fresh grapefruit juice**

1 teaspoon **grapefruit zest**

1 tablespoon **fresh mint**, chopped

Salt and freshly ground **black pepper** to taste

▶ **Combine** all ingredients except crab and lettuce in a bowl and **toss**.

▶ **Divide** lettuce between two plates and **top** with dressing mixture.

▶ **Arrange** crab on top of lettuce bed.

Variation: *You may top crab with Sautéed Shrimp Salad Dressing (page 49).*

Spinach Salad

2-4 Servings

1 12-16 ounce bag **baby spinach**

1/2 cup **pancetta** or bacon, chopped, cooked crisply, and drained

1/2 cup freshly grated **Parmesan cheese**

1/2 cup diced **tomatoes**

1 cup button **mushrooms**, sliced

1 cup **Croutons** (page 15)

1/4 cup green or red **onions**, finely chopped (optional)

1/2 cup **Marston's San Pasqual Dressing** (see Note)

▶ **Toss** all ingredients together and **divide** among chilled plates.

Variation: *Add fresh pomegranate seeds, goat cheese, and fresh satsuma oranges instead of bacon, Parmesan, and tomatoes.*

NOTE: *For a list of distributors of Marston's San Pasqual Dressing and other products, go to* **marstonproducts.com**.

Tomato Stuffed Artichoke

4 Servings

4 medium **artichokes**, steamed
8 medium **Roma tomatoes**, peeled and diced
1/2 cup **basil**, chopped
3 cloves **garlic**, finely chopped
1/2 cup **Panko bread crumbs** (or plain)
1 tablespoon **Dijon-style mustard**
3 tablespoons **balsamic vinegar**
1/2 cup **mayonnaise**
1 tablespoon freshly ground **black pepper**
3/4 cup freshly grated **Parmesan cheese**

▶ **Core** the cooked artichokes and **set aside** (make sure you remove all of the inside hair-like material; use a tablespoon to dig it out).

▶ **Combine** remaining ingredients and **stuff** mixture in cooked artichokes.

▶ **Refrigerate** for one hour and **serve**.

Variation: *Cook 3 to 4 large gulf shrimp per serving and serve warm on top of the artichoke.*

Dipping Sauce for Artichoke Leaves

3/4 cup **mayonnaise**
4 tablespoons **balsamic vinegar**
1 tablespoon **Dijon-style mustard**

▶ **Mix** all ingredients.

Watercress and Oak Leaf Lettuce Salad with Champagne Grapes

4 Servings

2 **tart green apples**, diced

1/2 cup **pine nuts**, toasted

2 bunches **watercress**, rinsed, dried, and stems removed

2 heads **baby oak leaf lettuce**, rinsed, dried, and torn

1 bunch **arugula**, rinsed and dried

1 cup **imported blue** or **goat cheese**, crumbled

4 small bunches **champagne grapes** (or other small grape varieties)

1/2 cup **Orange Vinaigrette**

▶ **Toss** all ingredients except grapes with dressing and **divide** among chilled plates.

▶ **Garnish** each plate with a small bunch of champagne grapes.

Orange Vinaigrette

1 cup **olive oil**

1/4 cup **rice wine vinegar**

1/4 cup **balsamic vinegar**

1/2 cup **fresh squeezed orange juice**

Salt and freshly ground **black pepper** to taste

▶ **Combine** all ingredients in blender and **mix** on high speed for 2 minutes until well blended.

Wild Rice and Chicken Salad
4 Servings

2 whole **chicken breasts** (4 halves), boned and skinned

2 tablespoons **chicken base**

8 cups **water**

2 cups **wild rice**

1 **red bell pepper**, seeded and julienned

1/2 **red onion**, finely chopped

4 **green onions**, chopped

1/2 cup **fresh mushrooms**, sliced

1 cup whole salted **cashews**

1 cup **fresh sugar snap peas**, deveined and blanched (place in boiling water for one minute, then cool in ice water)

1 cup bottled **soy ginger dressing**

1 head **butter** or **other lettuce**

- ▸ **Preheat** oven to 350 degrees.

- ▸ **Wrap** chicken breasts in foil and **bake** for 30 minutes. When cool, **chop** or shred.

- ▸ Bring chicken base and water to a **boil** and **add** rice. Reduce to **simmer**, cover and cook until done, about 30 minutes. **Drain** and set aside to cool.

- ▸ **Combine** red bell pepper, red and green onion, mushrooms, cashews, peas and dressing in a bowl and **toss** well.

- ▸ **Add** rice and chicken and **toss** well. **Cover** and **refrigerate** to chill, about 2 hours.

- ▸ **Serve** on bed of lettuce.

Sides, Sauces, and Toppings

Avocado Butter

Avocado Butter is an excellent flavor enhancer for fish or chicken.
Makes 1 cup

2 ripe **avocados**, diced
10 ounces **salted butter**, softened
1 teaspoon **Worcestershire sauce**
1/4 teaspoon **Tabasco sauce**
4 cloves **garlic**, finely minced
1 teaspoon freshly ground **black or white pepper**

▸ **Whisk** all ingredients together with wire whisk until smooth and thoroughly blended.

▸ **Roll** into log, **wrap** in waxed paper, and **chill** in refrigerator until ready to serve.

▸ **Slice** pieces of the log for each serving. You may also store in a bowl if you plan to serve the butter warm or at room temperature.

▸ **Store** in refrigerator up to 4 days.

Caramelized Onions

Makes 1 cup

4 **white or yellow onions**, peeled and thinly sliced

2 tablespoons **canola oil**

2 tablespoons **butter**

1 tablespoon **sugar**

1 teaspoon **chicken base**

1/2 cup **water**

▸ **Heat** oil and butter in heavy skillet over medium/low heat. **Add** onions, sugar, chicken base and water, and cook slowly, **stirring** frequently, for 40-60 minutes until onions are golden brown.

▸ **Store** refrigerated for up to a week and reheat as needed.

Variation: *See the Balsamic Caramelized Onion Reduction (page 122).*

Cherry Chutney

An excellent accompaniment to rack of lamb, beef, duck, or pork.
Makes 2 cups

3/4 cups **white sugar**

1/3 cup **cider vinegar**

1 tablespoon **fresh ginger**, peeled and minced

3 cloves **garlic**, minced

1 teaspoon ground **cumin**

1/2 teaspoon ground **cinnamon**

1/8 teaspoon crushed **dried red pepper**

1 large **red onion**, finely chopped

1 cup **dried cherries**

▸ **Combine** all ingredients in heavy sauce pan and **cook** over medium heat until mixture thickens, about 30 minutes.

▸ If you want a thinner sauce, you may **add** up to a cup of beef stock.

▸ **Store** refrigerated for up to a week.

A tip from Otis...
I recommend cooking "neat"—clean as you go so that knives, bowls, whisks, and other utensils are always ready for use!

Dill Sauce

This versatile sauce may be served hot or cold...ladled over salmon fillet or as a dip for cold shrimp.
Makes 1 cup

1 bunch **fresh dill**, finely chopped (tops only)

1 cup **whipping cream**

1 teaspoon **fresh lemon juice**

▸ **Combine** ingredients in small, heavy sauce pan and **reduce** over medium heat until thick, about 10 minutes.

▸ **Store** refrigerated for up to 4 days.

Guacamole

Makes 1 to 2 cups

2 large ripe **avocados**, diced

1/2 medium **red onion**, finely chopped

2 **Roma tomatoes**, diced

1 **jalapeño pepper**, seeded and finely diced

1/2 cup **cilantro**, coarsely chopped

1/2 **lemon** or whole **lime**, juiced

1 teaspoon **Worcestershire sauce**

Salt and freshly ground **black pepper** to taste

> **A tip from Otis...**
> To keep guacamole from turning brown, spread a thin layer of sour cream over the top.

▸ **Combine** all ingredients. **Mash** with fork if smoother consistency desired. May be refrigerated up to 3 days.

Grilled Vegetables
4 Servings

1 each **red** and **yellow bell pepper**, seeded and deveined
1 large **red onion**
1 bunch **asparagus**, trimmed
1 large **yellow squash**
1 large **zucchini**
1/2 cup **olive oil**
1 **lemon**, juiced
1 teaspoon **seasoned salt**

▸ **Wash** and **slice** vegetables lengthwise slices about 1/2 inch wide.

▸ **Whisk** together olive oil, lemon juice, and seasoned salt in small bowl.

▸ Lightly **coat** vegetables with oil mixture.

▸ **Grill** on barbecue, turning frequently until done.

▸ **Serve** immediately or refrigerate to serve cold.

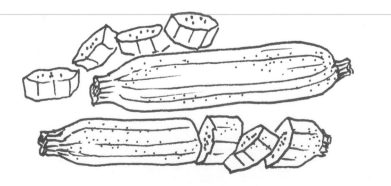

Honey Mustard Sauce

This sauce may be served cold—or serve it warm for best flavor. It's great on ham or turkey sandwiches or on dishes such as Crab Capellini (page 98).
Makes 1 cup

1 cup **honey**
1/4 cup **Dijon mustard**
1/4 cup **grainy mustard** (or more to taste)

▸ **Combine** all ingredients in small sauce pan.

▸ **Heat**, stirring constantly, just until blended.

▸ **Store** refrigerated for up to two weeks.

Marston's Candied Pecans

When Otis was chef at Marston's in Pasadena, you could find him in the kitchen at 5:45 each morning, making these fresh for the day's orders of California Orange and Cordierra Salad!
Makes 2 cups

2 cups **fresh pecan halves** (pieces are fine too)
3 cups **sugar**

▸ **Heat** sugar in large non-stick frying pan over medium heat. **Stir** frequently and watch closely until sugar melts.

▸ When all sugar has melted, **add** pecans and **stir** with two wooden spoons until all nuts are covered with sugar.

▸ **Pour** nut mixture onto cookie sheet that has been treated with cooking spray. **Spread** evenly while nuts are still warm.

▸ Before they are completely cooled, **remove** candied pecans from pan and **place** on chopping block or wooden cutting board. Using large knife, **cut** into small chunks.

▸ **Store** in airtight container at room temperature for up to four weeks.

Note: *For a list of distributors of Marston's Candied Pecans and other products, go to* **marstonproducts.com***.*

Onion Marmalade

This unique marmalade is a delicious addition to Otis's Meatloaf or try it as an appetizer, served with cream cheese and spread on crackers.
Makes about 1-1/2 cups

4 large **white onions**, peeled and thinly sliced

1/4 cup **sun dried tomatoes** (**Measure** dried tomatoes, then **soak** in water until soft, then finely chop.)

1 teaspoon **canned chipotle peppers**, finely chopped

1 cup **apricot jam**

▶ **Cook** onions, sun dried tomatoes and peppers in sauce pan over low heat for an hour.

▶ **Add** jam and cook another 5 minutes.

▶ **Serve** warm or at room temperature.

▶ **Store** refrigerated for up to one week.

Otis's Fabulous Dressing

Similar to a Caesar dressing, this Fabulous Dressing is great on any salad, but it goes particularly well with shrimp.
Makes 1/2 cup

1/4 cup **balsamic vinegar**

1/2 cup **olive** or **canola oil**

1 **coddled egg**

2 **garlic** cloves, minced

2 tablespoons **pickle relish**

1 teaspoon **Dijon-style mustard**

1 tablespoon **catsup**

Salt and freshly ground **black pepper** to taste

▶ **Combine** all ingredients in a blender, **mix** until smooth, and **chill**.

▶ **Store** refrigerated for up to 4 days.

Pesto Sauce

Great on pasta, spread on sandwiches, or as a side sauce for seafood!
Makes 1 cup

1/4 **pine nuts**, toasted

4 tablespoons **olive oil**

5 cloves **garlic**, minced

1/2 cup **basil leaves**, chopped and loosely packed

1/2 teaspoon freshly ground **black pepper**

1/4 teaspoon **salt**

1/2 cup freshly grated **Parmesan cheese**

▸ **Combine** all ingredients in a food processor and **blend** until smooth.

▸ **Store** refrigerated for up to one week.

Roasted Radicchio with Mozzarella

This is a delicious accompaniment to a fish or chicken entrée.
6 Servings

2 tablespoons **olive oil**

4 strips **bacon**, chopped and cooked

2 cloves **garlic**, thinly sliced

3 heads **radicchio**

1 cup **mozzarella** cheese, cubed

1/2 cup **Pecorino Romano** cheese, freshly grated

▸ **Preheat** oven to 400 degrees.

▸ Slowly **cook** olive oil, bacon and garlic over medium heat in small sauce pan. **Stir** occasionally and cook until bacon and garlic soften, about 5 minutes. Do not let garlic brown.

▸ **Rinse** heads of radicchio well in cold water and pat dry. **Cut** long heads in half lengthwise or round heads in quarters lengthwise.

▸ **Arrange** radicchio in baking pan and **pour** the garlic, oil, bacon mixture over it, **turning** to coat leaves evenly.

▸ **Bake** radicchio until soft, about 40 minutes, **turning** occasionally to keep coated with oil.

▸ **Remove** pan from oven, **distribute** mozzarella cubes over the top of the radicchio. **Sprinkle** the grated Romano cheese over all and return to oven.

▸ **Bake** until mozzarella melts and browns, about 3 minutes.

Shallot Caper Sauce

This sauce is perfect on chicken, fish, or pork...especially good on Crispy Salmon (page 100).
Makes 1 cup

1 large **shallot**, finely chopped

2 cloves **garlic**, finely chopped

2 tablespoons **butter**

1 teaspoon **chicken base**

2 tablespoons **capers** (or more if you prefer)

1 tablespoon **Dijon-style mustard**

1 cup **whipping cream**

1 teaspoon freshly ground **black pepper**

1/4 cup **fresh parsley**, chopped

▸ **Sauté** shallots and garlic in butter until soft.

▸ **Add** remaining ingredients except parsley. **Cook** over medium heat, **stirring** continually for about 15 minutes. **Thicken** with cornstarch paste if needed.

▸ **Add** parsley just before serving.

Spicy Fresh Salsa

A great dip for chips, garnish for soups, or topping for enchiladas, steak, or fish.
Makes 1 cup

3 large **tomatoes**, finely diced

2 **jalapeño peppers**, seeded and finely diced

1 bunch **cilantro**, washed and chopped

1 medium **red onion**, finely diced

1 tablespoon **Worcestershire sauce**

1 tablespoon fresh **lime juice**

Salt and freshly ground **black pepper** to taste

▸ **Mix** all ingredients together and chill.

▸ **Store** refrigerated for up to five days.

Spicy Tomato Jam

Serve with lamb, chicken or on barbecued hamburgers!
Makes 3 cups

1-1/4 cups **olive oil**
3 cups **white onion**, chopped
6 **garlic** cloves, minced
2 tablespoons **jalapeño peppers**, seeded and minced
3-1/2 pounds **plum tomatoes**, seeded and chopped
6 tablespoons **red wine vinegar**
2 tablespoons **sugar** (or more to taste)
1/2 cup fresh **cilantro**, chopped
Salt and freshly ground **black pepper**

▸ **Heat** oil in heavy pot, **add** onion, and **sauté** until soft. **Add** garlic, jalapeño, tomatoes, vinegar, and sugar.

▸ **Cook** for 30 minutes, **stirring** continually.

▸ **Add** cilantro and season with salt and pepper.

▸ Allow to **cool** before serving.

▸ **Store** refrigerated up to one week.

Bread, Beans, Potatoes, Pasta, and Rice

Baked Pumpernickel Croutons

A nice, crunchy topping for soups and salads.

8 slices **pumpernickel bread**
1/4 cup **olive oil** or **butter**
Cooking spray
1/4 cup **Parmesan cheese**
1 tablespoon **garlic salt**

▶ **Preheat** oven to 325 degrees.

▶ **Cut** bread into 1/4" chunks, leaving crust on.

▶ **Prepare** cookie sheet with cooking spray.

▶ **Lay** bread cubes on cookie sheet and **sprinkle** with garlic salt and Parmesan cheese and **toss** to coat evenly.

▶ **Drizzle** oil or butter over the bread.

▶ **Bake** until lightly crisped, about 30 minutes. **Stir** occasionally so all sides are toasted.

▶ **Cool** and **store** in airtight container up to two weeks.

Variations: *Rye, sourdough, or Kalamata olive bread also make great croutons.*

Beer Cheese Crostini

Yummy, hot, cheesy sourdough slices to serve with soups, salads, or as an appetizer!

1 pound **Cheddar cheese**, grated

12 ounces **beer** at room temperature

2 tablespoons **Worcestershire sauce**

1 teaspoon **Tabasco sauce**

1 teaspoon **dry mustard**

1 **sourdough** or **French** baguette, sliced

▸ **Preheat** oven to 400 degrees.

▸ **Process** all ingredients except bread in food processor; mixture should be chunky.

▸ **Spread** each bread slice with cheese mixture, **covering** each about 1/8 inch thick.

▸ **Bake** for about 6 minutes, until bubbly.

Black Beans

8 Servings

1 large **white onion**, chopped

3 cloves **garlic**, chopped

1/4 cup **olive oil**

2 tablespoons **chicken base**

16 cups **water**

4 cups **dried black beans** (washed and checked for pebbles)

1 tablespoon **Tabasco sauce**

1/2 cup **brown sugar**

▸ **Heat** olive oil in large soup pot and **sauté** onion and garlic until soft.

▸ **Add** all other ingredients and **boil** for about 60 minutes on medium heat or until beans are soft.

Serving Suggestions: *Serve warm with barbecued meat, chicken, fish, enchiladas, or stuffed peppers. Black beans also add a nice texture to salads when served cold.*

Black Beans and Rice

A great side dish or vegetarian entrée.
8-10 Servings

1 recipe **Black Beans**

2 cups **white rice**

4 cups **water**

4 medium **carrots**, finely chopped

1 large **white onion**, finely chopped

1 cup **Spicy Fresh Salsa** (page70) or purchased salsa

1 cup **Cheddar cheese**, grated

1 cup **Monterey Jack cheese**, grated

▸ **Prehea**t oven to 375 degrees.

▸ **Boil** water, add rice, carrots, and onions. Turn to **simmer**, cover, and cook until done, about 20-30 minutes.

▸ **Stir** salsa into rice mixture.

▸ In 9"x13" baking dish, **layer** black beans, rice, and cheeses. **Repeat** layers.

▸ **Bake** uncovered until cheese is melted, about 20-30 minutes.

Cheddar Cheese Popovers

A basket of these warm little biscuits makes soup or salad a meal.
Makes approximately 32

1/4 pound **butter**

2 cups **milk**

12 **eggs**, lightly beaten

3-1/2 cups **flour**

1 teaspoon **Cajun spice**

1/4 teaspoon **cayenne pepper**

1/4 teaspoon freshly ground **black pepper**

Cooking spray

1/2 cup grated **Cheddar cheese**

▸ **Preheat** oven to 375 degrees.

▸ **Melt** butter in saucepan over medium heat. **Remove** from heat and **stir** in milk and eggs, **mixing** well with a whisk.

▸ **Add** flour, Cajun spice, cayenne and black peppers. **Mix** well.

▸ **Coat** miniature muffin tins — Teflon is best — with cooking spray. **Spoon** mixture into tins. **Sprinkle** grated cheese on top.

▸ **Bake** for 35 minutes, or until tops are golden brown.

▸ **Serve** warm.

Variations: *Instead of Cheddar, top with blue, Gouda, Swiss or Fontina cheese.*

Cheesy Garlic Bread

Great with any soup or salad.

1 pound **mozzarella cheese**, grated
1 pound **Cheddar cheese**, grated
3/4 pound **butter**, softened
1 cup freshly grated **Parmesan cheese**
4 cloves of **garlic**, minced
1 tablespoon **Worcestershire sauce**
1 large loaf **sourdough bread**, cut in half lengthwise

▸ **Preheat** oven to 375 degrees.

▸ **Combine** all ingredients to make cheese mixture and **spread** on both halves of bread.

▸ **Wrap** each half in foil and **bake** until bread is hot about 15 minutes.

▸ **Fold** foil back and **broil** until lightly browned.

▸ **Cut** into serving pieces and **serve** while hot.

Four Cheese Macaroni

A great vegetarian dinner or side dish!
6 Servings

3/4 pound **elbow** or **penne pasta**

1/4 cup **butter**

1 cup **onion**, diced

1/2 cup **Caramelized Onions** (page 59, optional but an excellent addition!)

1/2 cup **flour**

3 cups **milk**

1/4 cup **Parmesan cheese**, grated

1-1/2 cups **white Cheddar cheese**, grated (reserve 1/2 cup for topping)

1 cup **sharp Cheddar cheese**, grated

2 tablespoons **Dijon-style mustard**

Dash of **nutmeg**

Salt and freshly ground **black pepper** to taste

1 teaspoon **chicken base**

6 ounces **goat cheese**

▷ **Preheat** oven to 400 degrees.

▷ **Cook** pasta in lightly salted water until al dente, about 10 minutes. Do not overcook — it will cook more in the oven. **Drain**, **rinse** with warm water and **set aside** in large bowl.

▷ **Melt** butter in large saucepan. **Add** onions and **cook** over medium heat about 5 minutes.

▷ **Stir** in flour and **cook** 3 more minutes.

▷ Gradually **add** milk, **stirring** until thickened.

▷ **Add** Cheddar cheeses and **stir** until melted.

▷ **Add** mustard, nutmeg, salt, pepper, and chicken base. **Reduce** heat and **cook** an additional 3 minutes, **stirring** constantly.

▷ **Pour** cheese mixture over pasta; **fold** in caramelized onions, and **mix** well to coat. **Pour** into buttered, shallow, baking dish or casserole.

▷ **Top** with Parmesan, 1/2 reserved cheddar, and dot with goat cheese and Caramelized Onions (optional).

▷ **Bake** uncovered for 20-30 minutes, until lightly browned and bubbly.

Fresh Spinach Mashed Potatoes

A cozy winter dish served alongside Otis's meatloaf (page 112)!
8 Servings

8 **russet potatoes**, washed and quartered with skin left on

2 cloves **garlic**, minced

1 bunch **fresh spinach**, washed well, stemmed, and chopped

1/4 pound **butter**

3/4 cup **low-fat milk**

A dash of **nutmeg**

Salt and pepper to taste

▸ **Boil** potatoes in water with half of the minced garlic. **Cook** over medium high heat for about 30 minutes until done.

▸ While potatoes are cooking, **sauté** the spinach over medium heat in two tablespoons of the butter and the remaining garlic. **Cook** about 3 minutes, or just until spinach is soft.

▸ When potatoes are done, **drain** and **whip** with an electric mixer or hand beater, **adding** the milk and remaining butter. When mixed and fluffy, **stir** in spinach and **add** nutmeg, salt, and pepper.

Variation: *Omit the spinach and add 1/2 cup Gorgonzola cheese or blue cheese.*

Jalapeño Corn Bread Bowl

You can serve a basket of the corn bread with chili or create a main dish in a bowl!
8 Servings

1 box **corn bread mix** (6-8 ounces)

1 cup **corn** — cut fresh off the cob is best, but canned and drained or frozen is fine

3 medium **jalapeño peppers**, seeded and finely diced

4 cups **Black Beans** (page 76)

2 cups **Spicy Fresh Salsa** (page 70)

1 cup **sour cream**

2 **avocados**, coarsely chopped

2 cups **Monterey Jack** or **Cheddar cheese**, grated

▸ **Preheat** oven to 375 degrees.

▸ **Make** corn bread according to directions, **adding** corn and jalapeño peppers to the mix.

▸ While corn bread is baking, **gather** other ingredients and **heat** the black beans.

▸ **Cut** generous pieces of corn bread, **slice** in half horizontally, and **place** each in a large soup bowl or on a plate.

▸ **Ladle** 1/2 cup of black beans over each bottom piece.

▸ **Place** corn bread top on each. **Sprinkle** Monterey Jack or Cheddar cheese on top of each serving and **put under broiler** to melt cheese

▸ **Garnish** with a spoonful of salsa, sour cream and chopped avocado..

Macadamia Nut Pancakes

2 cups **Krusteaz Buttermilk Pancake Mix**
2 cups **water**
1-1/2 cups roasted and salted **macadamia nuts**, finely chopped
Butter for cooking and serving on side
Warm **maple syrup**

▸ **Blend** pancake mix and water. **Let sit** for 30 minutes. **Stir** again.

▸ **Ladle** pancake mix onto hot buttered griddle.

▸ **Sprinkle** a generous portion of nuts on each pancake.

▸ **Turn** pancakes over when batter bubbles and finish cooking.

▸ **Top** with more nuts and **serve** with melted butter and warm maple syrup.

Marston's Famous Blueberry Pancakes

This is a simple recipe, but what makes these crepe-like pancakes delicious are the wild Maine Blueberries. You should be able to find them canned in the specialty food aisle.

Krusteaz Pancake Mix
Canned Wild Maine Blueberries (these are best, but others will do)
Oil
Butter
Warm **maple syrup**

▶ **Make** pancake mix using 1 cup mix to 1 cup water. **Allow** to sit for 30 minutes, **whipping** twice.

▶ **Rinse** and drain blueberries.

▶ **Add** blueberries to pancake mix and ladle onto lightly oiled, hot griddle.

▶ **Cook** until batter bubbles, then **flip** and **cook** until done.

▶ **Serve** immediately with butter and warm maple syrup. Leftover mix may be kept refrigerated for up to three days.

Marston's Fantastic French Toast with Banana Sauté

Sinfully delicious and easy breakfast fare "toasted" by food critics across Southern California and Gourmet magazine!
6-8 Servings

8 1-inch-thick slices **sourdough bread**, halved (you may use thinner bread)

6 **eggs**, lightly beaten

1 teaspoon **vanilla**

4 cups **corn flakes cereal**, lightly crushed

2 teaspoons **ground cinnamon**

Butter for cooking

Powdered sugar

Banana Sauté (recipe follows)

Suggested garnishes: melted butter, powdered sugar, lemon wedges, warm maple syrup, warm berry jam, fresh berries

▸ **Mix** eggs and vanilla, **pour** into baking dish and **set aside**.

▸ **Toss** crushed corn flakes and cinnamon and **pour** onto plate.

▸ **Dip** each piece of bread in egg mixture. **Soak** very well, then **dredge** in corn flake mixture, coating both sides.

▸ **Cook** on well-buttered griddle or heavy skillet over medium heat until golden brown.

▸ **Fan** slices on a serving platter, **sprinkle** with powdered sugar and **serve** with Banana Sauté and the toppings of your choice.

Note: *When serving for a brunch you may keep slices of French toast warm on a cookie tray in a 250 degree oven for up to 30 minutes.*

Banana Sauté

1/2 cup **brown sugar**

3 **bananas**, sliced

2 tablespoons **rum or Grand Marnier**

▶ **Melt** sugar in frying pan.

▶ **Add** sliced bananas and **cook** about 5 minutes.

▶ **Add** rum or Grand Marnier.

▶ **Serve** on side or ladle on French toast or plain pancakes.

Spicy Baked Beans
A great side dish for Baby Back Ribs!
8-10 Servings

4 **white onions**, sliced

4 tablespoons **butter**

3/4 cup **brown sugar**

1 tablespoon canned **chipolte peppers in adobo sauce**, finely chopped (or less, it's spicy!)

4 tablespoons **maple syrup**

2 tablespoons **Dijon-style mustard**

1-3/4 cups **catsup**

1 24 ounce can of **Bush baked beans** (other brands are fine, too)

1 pound **bacon**, chopped, cooked, and drained

▸ **Preheat** oven to 375 degrees.

▸ **Sauté** onions in butter over medium heat for about 10 minutes.

▸ **Mix** brown sugar, peppers, syrup, mustard and catsup together in a bowl.

▸ **Place** beans and bacon in a casserole dish. **Add** onion and brown sugar mixture and **stir** well to combine ingredients.

▸ **Bake** covered for one hour.

Spicy White Corn with Cilantro

This versatile dish can be served hot or cold on its own, tossed with greens for salad, atop quesadillas or as a garnish with steak or fish.
4 Servings

1 tablespoon **olive oil**

4 ears **white corn** (about 4 cups), cut off the cob (or use canned white corn, drained)

1 **jalapeño pepper**, seeded and finely diced (2 peppers for a spicier salad)

1/2 teaspoon **salt**

2 teaspoons **Champagne wine vinegar**

4 teaspoons **fresh lime juice**

Dash **cayenne pepper**

1/2 bunch **cilantro**, washed and chopped

1 **green onion** (white and tops), sliced diagonally

1 cup **cherry tomatoes**, halved

▸ **Heat** the olive oil in a large skillet. **Add** the corn, jalapeño pepper, and 1/4 teaspoon salt. **Sauté** over medium heat for about 8 minutes, until the corn is just tender.

▸ **Transfer** to a bowl and **toss** the warm corn with the vinegar, lime juice, remaining 1/4 teaspoon salt, and cayenne pepper.

▸ When the corn is cool, **add** the cilantro and sliced scallion. For a spicier salad, **add** more cayenne or another jalapeño pepper.

▸ **Toss** in cherry tomatoes just before serving.

Swiss Scalloped Yams

A perfect side for Macadamia Nut Encrusted Halibut or other fish entrée.
6 Servings

4-5 large **yams**
4 tablespoons **butter**, melted
Salt and freshly ground **black pepper** to taste
1 large **white onion**, chopped
1 cup **whipping cream**
2 cups **Swiss cheese**, grated (or mixture of Swiss and Fontina)

▸ **Preheat** oven to 375 degrees.

▸ **Bake** whole yams just until soft when pricked with fork, about 35 minutes. **Reduce** oven temperature to 350 degrees.

▸ When cool enough to handle, **peel** and **slice** the yams in 1/8" slices.

▸ In a baking pan, **layer** yams, melted butter, salt, pepper, onion, whipping cream, and Swiss Cheese. **Repeat** layers twice, ending with cheese on top.

▸ **Bake** uncovered for about 30-40 minutes.

▸ **Broil** for a few minutes to brown top.

Wild Rice with Apples and Portobello Mushrooms

For an elegant dinner party, serve this with Roast Duck and Kiwi Sauce (page 118).
4 Servings

2 cups **wild rice**

2 tablespoons **chicken base** (or more to taste)

1 cup **Portobello mushrooms**, sliced

5 tablespoons **butter**

Salt and freshly ground **black pepper**

2 **green apples**, finely chopped

1 tablespoon **cider vinegar**

1 teaspoon **sugar**

▶ **Bring** 6 cups of water to a **boil**, **add** rice and 2 tablespoons of the chicken base and **bring** back to a boil. **Cover** and **simmer** until rice is done, about 40-60 minutes. **Taste** to be sure rice is done; if underdone, it will be too chewy. After rice is cooked, **pour** off any excess liquid.

▶ **Sauté** mushrooms in 3 tablespoons of the butter for about 10 minutes. **Add** salt and pepper to taste.

▶ **Sauté** apples in remaining 2 tablespoons butter, cider vinegar and sugar. **Cook** until apples are just soft, about 5 minutes.

▶ **Combine** rice, mushrooms, and apples and **keep warm** in a covered casserole dish.

▶ **Serve** loose or make individual portions with a small mold, using a small tin can for a mold. **Stuff** rice in mold and pack tightly, then **unmold** carefully.

Entrées

Baby Back Ribs Texas Style

Yummy with Spicy Baked Beans (page 88). These ribs may be made ahead and refrigerated for up to three days. To serve, reheat, add some barbecue sauce and bake in oven or on the grill.
4 Servings

2 racks **baby back pork ribs**

1/2 cup **fresh lemon juice**

2 cups bottled **barbecue sauce** (Bullseye is good)

1 teaspoon **Cajun spice**

Salt and freshly ground **black pepper** to taste

▸ **Preheat** oven to 325 degrees

▸ **Combine** lemon juice, barbecue sauce, Cajun spice, salt and pepper in a small bowl.

▸ **Place** ribs in baking pan, **spread** both sides with sauce, and **cover** pan with foil.

▸ **Bake** for 1-1/2 to 2 hours at 325 degrees, or until done. They should be so tender that the meat falls off the bone! **Serve** with lots of napkins!

Bratwurst and Caramelized Onions

4 Servings

8 **bratwurst sausages**, 2-4 ounces each
2 bottles of your favorite **beer**
2 cups **Caramelized Onions** (page 59)
1 large **white onion**, chopped

▸ **Preheat** oven to 350 degrees.

▸ **Marinate** sausage, onion, and caramelized onion in beer for 30 minutes,

▸ **Transfer** to baking pan and **bake** uncovered for 30 minutes.

▸ **Serve** on crusty sourdough rolls with spicy brown mustard.

‖●‖ Corned Beef Hash

This was an occasional breakfast special at Marston's...a favorite of our regular customers. It's even better the second day!
6 Servings

1 4-pound **corned beef brisket**

8 cups **water**

5 medium **potatoes**, diced, skin on

2 each **green** and **red bell peppers**, seeded and chopped

2 medium **red onions**, chopped

2 cloves **garlic**, finely chopped

2 tablespoons **vegetable oil**

1 teaspoon **salt**

1/2 teaspoon freshly ground **black pepper**

4 cups **water**

2 tablespoons **beef base**

1 tablespoon freshly ground **black pepper**

1 tablespoons **Worcestershire sauce**

1/4 cup **red wine**

Cornstarch paste

6 **eggs** for topping

▶ **Preheat** oven to 375 degrees.

▶ Bring water to a **boil** and **add** beef brisket. **Add** more water if necessary to completely cover brisket. **Turn** to slow boil and cook until tender, about 2-3 hours.

▶ **Remove** brisket from water, remove all fat, **shred** brisket into strips, and **chop** in small pieces.

▶ **Combine** diced potatoes, green and red bell peppers, onions and garlic. **Toss** with vegetable oil, salt and pepper, **place** in baking dish, **cover** with foil and bake for 30 minutes. Do not overcook!

▶ **Make** gravy by combining 4 cups water, beef base, pepper, Worcestershire sauce, and wine. **Simmer** for 5 minutes then **add** cornstarch paste and stir until thickened. You may not need to use all of this mixture...only as needed to bind the patties

▶ **Combine** beef brisket with potato/pepper mixture and **moisten** with gravy. **Shape** into 6-ounce patties and **fry** in butter, cooking both sides until crisp.

▶ **Serve** with poached or fried eggs on top of each serving.

Crab Capellini with Honey Mustard Sauce

At Marston's, we served this popular luncheon dish with Jicama Salad. Miniature patties make great appetizers!
6-8 Servings

3/4 pound **fresh capellini** or angel hair pasta

1-1/2 pounds **fresh crab**, chopped or shredded (you can use imitation crab)

3 cloves **garlic**, finely chopped

1/2 **red bell pepper**, finely diced

1/2 **green bell pepper**, finely diced

3 **scallions**, white and tops, finely chopped

1/4 teaspoon freshly ground **black pepper**

1/4 teaspoon **Cajun seasoning**

3/4 cup freshly grated **Parmesan cheese**

2 **eggs**, lightly beaten

3 tablespoons **olive oil** or **butter**

1 **avocado**, sliced for topping

Honey Mustard Sauce (page 63)

▶ **Preheat** oven to 350 degrees.

▶ **Break** pasta in half and cook in salted water until al dente, about 5 minutes. **Rinse** with cold water; **drain**.

▶ **Mix** pasta together with all remaining ingredients. Make into 4" patties about 1/2" thick.

▶ **Heat** olive oil or butter in a heavy skillet and **brown** crab patties, about 5 minutes per side or until cooked through.

▶ **Remove** to baking pan and **bake** for about 10 minutes at 350 degrees.

▶ **Serve** topped with a slice of avocado and Honey Mustard Sauce.

Crispy Salmon with Shallot Caper Sauce and Fresh Corn Succotash

This was the centerpiece of a memorable family reunion feast prepared by Otis in Central Oregon. Served with Gorgonzola Mashed Potatoes (page 82), Fresh Corn Succotash, and Caesar Salad (page 42), Otis had 16 family members oohing and ahhing!
4 Servings

4 7-ounce **salmon fillets**, skinned

1 cup **sugar**

1 recipe **Shallot Caper Sauce** (page 69)

▸ **Preheat** oven to 375 degrees.

▸ **Rinse** salmon and **pat dry**.

▸ **Press** generous portion of sugar on all sides of salmon fillets.

▸ **Heat** dry frying pan to medium-high heat. **Sauté** salmon and keep **turning** until crisp and brown. Be prepared for your kitchen to get a bit smoky during this process!

▸ When each piece is crispy, **place** on cookie sheet that has been sprayed with cooking spray.

▸ **Bake** in oven to finish cooking, about 7-10 minutes. Do not overcook!

▸ **Top** with Shallot Caper Sauce and serve on a bed of warm Fresh Corn Succotash.

Fresh Corn Succotash

4 tablespoons **butter** or **oil**

1 **shallot**, finely diced

1 small **red onion**, finely diced

4 cloves **garlic**, minced

1 each **red** and **green bell pepper**, seeded and finely diced

1 **Anaheim pepper**, seeded and finely diced

1 small **jalapeño pepper**, seeded, for spicy flavor (optional)

1/2 pound **bacon** or **Canadian bacon**, cooked, and diced

6 ears **fresh corn**, white or yellow

1 16-ounce bag **frozen corn**

1/2 pound **bacon** or **Canadian bacon**, diced, and cooked

Salt and freshly ground **black pepper**

▶ **Sauté** shallot, onion, and garlic in butter or oil.

▶ **Add** peppers and continue to **sauté** about 3 minutes.

▶ **Add** corn and continue **cooking** about 10 minutes until corn is done.

▶ **Stir** in bacon, **season** with salt and pepper, and **serve**.

Filet Mignon with Portobello Mushroom Sauce

Serve over a bed of Fresh Spinach Mashed Potatoes (page 82) for a meat lover's meal!

8 Servings

8 10-ounce **filet mignon steaks**, all side fat removed

4 tablespoons **butter**

2 cloves **garlic**, diced

3 **shallots**, diced

Portobello Mushroom Sauce (recipe follows)

▸ **Sauté** steaks in butter in large frying pan until done as desired (about 20 minutes for medium rare, depending on thickness)

▸ **Add** garlic and shallots to the pan and cook about 5 minutes.

▸ **Remove** steaks from pan and **pour** prepared Portobello Mushroom Sauce into pan. **Stir** with wire whisk, picking up all the pan juices and tidbits. This makes the sauce taste richer. **Return** filets to pan with sauce and **reheat**.

▸ **Remove** steaks from pan and **pour** sauce over steaks to serve.

> **A tip from Otis...**
>
> If you use sun dried tomatoes in oil, rinse them first, then chop them. If tomatoes are dry, boil them in a small amount of water to soften, drain and chop them.

Portobello Mushroom Sauce

3 tablespoons **butter**
2 large **Portobello mushrooms** (about 8 ounces total) stems removed, finely chopped
1 **shallot**, finely diced
2 tablespoons **sun dried tomatoes**, finely chopped
1/2 cup **whipping cream**
1 teaspoon **Dijon-style mustard**
Salt and freshly ground **black pepper** to taste

▶ **Heat** butter in a medium sauce pan and **sauté** mushrooms and shallots.

▶ **Add** tomatoes and whipping cream and bring to a **slow boil**.

▶ **Turn** heat to low, **add** mustard, salt and pepper. **Mix** thoroughly and remove from heat.

Herb Crusted Rosemary Pork Roulade

The Wild Rice with Apples and Portobello Mushrooms (page 91) makes a nice side dish.
4 Servings

1-1/2 pounds **boneless pork loin**, butterflied and pounded to 1/4" thick

1 tablespoon grated **lemon rind**

3 tablespoons **fresh parsley**, finely chopped

2 cloves **garlic**, minced

1 tablespoon **fresh rosemary**, minced

3 whole **rosemary sprigs**

1 teaspoon **salt**

1 teaspoon freshly ground **black pepper**

2 teaspoons **olive oil**

2 teaspoons **soy sauce**

2 tablespoons **butter**

1 cup **red wine**

1 cup **beef stock** (canned, homemade, or make with beef base)

4 tablespoons **butter**, chilled

▸ **Mix** lemon rind, parsley, garlic, minced rosemary, salt, and pepper to make the herb mixture.

▸ **Lay** pork flat and rub herb mixture into meat. **Roll** pork to form a roulade and **tie** with kitchen twine every two inches. **Tuck** rosemary sprigs under strings.

▸ **Place** roulade in roasting pan and **drizzle** with olive oil and soy sauce. **Cover** and **marinate** in refrigerator for 2 hours.

- **Preheat** oven to 450 degrees .

- **Remove** roulade from marinade and **brown** in hot skillet with 2 tablespoons butter for 5 minutes. **Place** in roasting pan.

- **Roast** pork for 20 minutes at 450 degrees, then **reduce heat** to 325 and **continue roasting** for 15 minutes, basting twice, until internal temperature of meat is 155 degrees. Meat should be slightly pink when done.

- **Remove** roulade to serving platter and **cover** with foil to keep warm.

- **Deglaze** roasting pan with red wine, **cooking** about 5 minutes to **reduce** by half.

- **Add** beef stock and cook about 5-10 minutes to **reduce** by half. **Whisk** in butter until melted.

- **Carve** pork in thin slices and **top** with sauce.

A tip from Otis...

After meat (or other food) has been sautéed and the meat and excess fat removed from the pan, deglaze the pan by adding a small amount of liquid (wine or stock), stirring to loosen the browned bits of meat on the bottom. The resulting mixture becomes the base for a sauce to accompany the meat.

Macadamia Encrusted Halibut with Sun Dried Tomato Sauce

Swiss Scalloped Yams (page 90) make a great side dish.
4 Servings

4 7-ounce fresh **halibut steaks**

1/2 cup **macadamia nuts**, finely chopped

1/2 cup **Panko bread crumbs** (in Asian section of your market)

2 tablespoons **fresh parsley**, finely chopped

1/2 teaspoon **salt**

1/2 teaspoon freshly ground **black pepper**

2 tablespoons **olive oil**

2 tablespoons **butter**

1/2 cup **Parmesan cheese**, freshly grated

▸ **Moisten** halibut with water.

▸ **Toss** macadamia nuts, bread crumbs, parsley, salt, and pepper together and **coat** the halibut steaks on both sides with mixture.

▸ **Heat** olive oil and butter in large skillet and **brown** halibut on both sides.

▸ **Place** browned halibut steaks in baking dish and **finish cooking** in 375 degree oven for 10 minutes, uncovered.

▸ **Sprinkle** with Parmesan cheese and **broil** until lightly browned.

▸ **Top** with Sun Dried Tomato Sauce

Variation: *Instead of halibut, use chicken breasts and dip in egg wash (1 egg and 2 tablespoons water, mixed) before coating with spices.*

Sun Dried Tomato Sauce

10 **Kalamata olives**, pitted

1 cup **sun dried tomatoes** (washed and drained if using tomatoes packed in oil or softened in boiling water for a few minutes if using dried)

2 **garlic** cloves, minced

3 tablespoons **olive oil**

1 tablespoon **fresh basil**, finely chopped

Salt and freshly ground **black pepper** to taste

▸ **Place** all ingredients in food processor and **process** until still chunky.

▸ **Heat** to serving temperature and **spoon** sauce over halibut.

A tip from Otis...
Because the water content of fish is so high, it dries out quickly when cooking. Check inside the thickest part of the fish to test for doneness.

Macadamia Encrusted White Fish with Mango Mayonnaise
4 Servings

4 7-ounce **white fish filets**, skinned
Salt and freshly ground **black pepper**
1 pound **macadamia nuts**, chopped
2 tablespoons **olive oil**
2 tablespoons **butter**

▸ **Preheat** oven to 375 degrees.

▸ **Rinse** fish in cold water and **pat dry**. Lightly **season** with salt and pepper and **dredge** in chopped nuts. **Refrigerate** for one hour.

▸ **Heat** olive oil and butter in large skillet and **brown** fish on both sides.

▸ **Place** in uncovered baking pan and **finish cooking** in oven for about 5 minutes or until done. Fish should be moist and flaky with even white color.

▸ **Serve** topped with Mango Mayonnaise

Variation: *Use Panko bread crumbs instead of macadamia nuts.*

Mango Mayonnaise

This is an excellent topping for salmon, swordfish, ahi, and fried clams.

2 **fresh mangoes**, peeled and chopped

1 **jalapeño pepper**, seeded and finely chopped

1/2 cup **cilantro**, chopped

1/2 cup **red bell pepper**, finely chopped

2 **scallions** (whites and tops), finely chopped

1/2 **red onion**, finely chopped

1/2 cup **mayonnaise**

1 teaspoon freshly ground **black pepper**

▶ **Combine** all ingredients except mayonnaise and **mix** thoroughly.

▶ **Add** mayonnaise and mix. **Serve** at room temperature.

▶ Mayonnaise can be **stored** in the refrigerator up to 4 days.

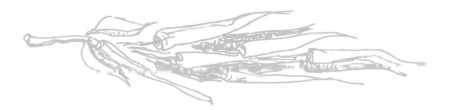

Muffuletta Sandwich with Pepperoncini Dressing

Great tailgater fare! A specialty of New Orleans, this hero-style sandwich originated in 1906 at the Central Grocery.
2 Large or 4 Small Servings

2 **French dip rolls** (or try sour dough, rosemary olive or other breads)

2 ounces thinly sliced **beef**

2 ounces thinly sliced **ham, salami,** and/or **turkey**

2 slices **Fontina cheese**

2 slices **Cheddar cheese**

4 slices **red onion**

4 slices **tomato**

2 pieces **lettuce**

Pepperoncini Dressing (recipe follows)

2 tablespoons **mayonnaise**

▶ **Preheat** oven to 375 degrees.

▶ **Cut** rolls in half lengthwise and **remove** soft dough.

▶ **Layer** all ingredients in each roll, **adding** the cheeses between the meats.

▶ **Spread** each roll with about 4 tablespoons Pepperoncini Dressing and 1 tablespoon mayonnaise.

▶ **Wrap** each sandwich in foil and **bake** for 20 minutes.

▶ **Remove** from oven, **unwrap**, **cut** each sandwich in half, and **serve**.

Pepperoncini Dressing

This is great as a sandwich spread or with bread for a meal in place of butter.

10 **Kalamata olives**, pitted

8 **pepperoncinis**, stemmed

4 **garlic** cloves

1/2 cup **olive oil**

3 **dill pickle** spears

▸ **Place** all ingredients in food processor and **mix** briefly. Dressing should have a slightly chunky texture.

▸ **Refrigerate** until ready to use.

Vegetarian Variation for the Muffuletta Sandwich

1 roasted **red bell pepper**

1 **avocado**, sliced thinly

1/4 **red onion**, sliced

1/4 cup **black olives**, sliced (may use green, too)

4 **marinated artichoke hearts**, sliced

1/2 **tomato**, sliced

4 ounces **goat cheese**

8 **spinach leaves**

▸ **Assemble** according to directions for Muffuletta Sandwich for a delicious vegetarian treat!

⚙ Otis's Meatloaf with Tomato Barbecue Sauce

This old fashioned dish was inspired by Otis's mother-in-law, Margaret Newport. Serve with Fresh Spinach Mashed Potatoes (page 82). Make gravy by adding beef broth to the pan juices.
8 Servings

3 tablespoons **olive oil**

1 **red onion**, finely chopped

2 cloves **garlic**, minced

1 **red bell pepper** chopped

2 stalks **celery**, finely chopped

1/2 cup **carrots**, finely chopped

1/2 cup **black olives**, chopped

3 pounds **ground beef**

1/2 cup **Worcestershire sauce**

1/2 cup **barbecue sauce** (bottled is fine)

1/2 cup **Panko bread crumbs** (regular are fine too)

2 **eggs**, beaten

Salt and freshly ground **black pepper**

4 strips **bacon**

Tomato Barbecue Sauce (recipe follows)

▶ **Preheat** oven to 350 degrees.

▶ **Heat** olive oil in skillet and **sauté** onion, garlic, pepper, celery and carrots for 15 minutes. **Add** black olives.

▶ In a large mixing bowl, **combine** sautéed vegetables, beef, Worcestershire and barbecue sauces, bread crumbs, eggs, salt and pepper. It's easiest to **mix** this thoroughly with your hands; **form** a loaf.

▸ **Place** meatloaf in 9"x13" baking pan. **Lay** uncooked bacon strips over the top and **cook** for 30 minutes.

▸ **Drain** off fat and **pour** Tomato Barbecue Sauce over the meatloaf.

▸ **Cook** an additional 30-40 minutes or until done. **Let stand** for 10 minutes, covered, to set.

Variation: *Use leftover meatloaf to create a great sandwich! Lightly grill sourdough, add a slice of grilled meatloaf, red onion, and cheddar cheese, then a final heating on the grill. For a spicy flavor, top with Chipolte mayonnaise, made with 1/3 cup mayonnaise and two finely chopped canned chipolte peppers.*

Tomato Barbecue Sauce

3/4 cup **barbecue sauce**

1/4 cup **catsup**

1/2 cup **brown sugar**

3 tablespoons **mustard**

▸ **Heat** all ingredients in saucepan. **Serve** warm as a side sauce or **pour** over meatloaf halfway through baking.

Phyllo Dough Wrapped Chicken Breast with Goat Cheese Sauce
4 Servings

1/2 cup **butter**

2 whole **chicken breasts**, halved, boned and skinned

1/2 bunch **fresh spinach**, washed

8 pieces **prosciutto ham**, thinly sliced

1/2 cup **Caramelized Onions** (page 59)

8 **phyllo dough sheets**, cut in half

Goat Cheese Sauce (recipe follows)

Suggested garnishes: 1/2 **red bell pepper**, seeded, julienned, and lightly sautéed in butter, 2 tablespoons **chives**, chopped

▶ **Preheat** oven to 375 degrees.

▶ **Heat** 1/4 cup of the butter in large skillet and **sauté** chicken breasts until chicken is lightly browned.

▶ **Remove** from pan and **place** 5-6 spinach leaves, 2 pieces of ham, and a portion of caramelized onions on each breast.

▶ **Wrap** each chicken breast in 1/2 sheet of phyllo dough **brushed** with melted butter. **Repeat** and **place** on greased cookie sheet.

▶ **Brush** each phyllo packet with melted butter.

▶ **Bake** for 30 minutes.

▶ **Serve** with Goat Cheese Sauce and **garnish** with red pepper and chives.

Goat Cheese Sauce

2 **shallots**, finely chopped

2 cups **white wine**

6 whole **black peppercorns**

1 tablespoon, **fresh tarragon**, chopped

1/2 cup **whipping cream**

1 12-ounce log of **goat cheese**

Salt and freshly ground **black pepper** to taste

▸ **Place** shallots, wine, peppercorns, and tarragon in heavy sauce pan over medium heat. **Reduce** liquid by three-fourths. **Strain** and **pour** liquid back into pan.

▸ **Add** whipping cream and bring to a **low boil**, stirring frequently.

▸ **Add** goat cheese in small pieces and stir with whisk.

▸ **Thicken** mixture if necessary with cornstarch paste.

Rack of Lamb

4 Servings

1 **rack of lamb** (approximately 16 chops)*
1/4 cup **olive oil**
1 cup **Panko bread crumbs**
1/4 cup **fresh rosemary**, chopped
8 cloves **garlic**, finely chopped
1/4 pound **butter**, melted
8 tablespoons **Dijon-style mustard**
Salt and freshly ground **black pepper** to taste
Au Jus (recipe follows)

▶ **Preheat** oven to 400 degrees.

▶ **Heat** olive oil in a large skillet and **brown** the lamb on both sides to give the meat some color.

▶ **Combine** bread crumbs, rosemary, garlic and butter.

▶ **Spread** mustard on both sides of lamb. **Pat** bread crumb mixture on lamb rack and **lay** rack in baking pan.

▶ **Bake** uncovered for 20-30 minutes. Lamb tastes best if cooked medium rare, but if you prefer it well-done, cook about 15 minutes longer.

▶ **Cut** chops, **arrange** on plate and **ladle** Au Jus on top.

Ask your butcher to remove the fat cap and french (clean lamb) to the eye.

Au Jus

2 cups **water**

2 tablespoons **beef base**

1 teaspoon **Worcestershire sauce**

1 teaspoon **Dijon-style mustard**

2 tablespoons **merlot** or **cabernet sauvignon** wine

▸ **Combine** all ingredients in sauce pan and bring to low boil. **Cook** until reduced by a little more than half.

Serving suggestion: *Alternate chops and slices of Polenta (page 122) on serving platter. Ladle Au Jus over top and pass a bowl of Cherry Chutney (page 60) to complete this dinner party dish!*

Otis's Tips

If you leave the lid off the pan when you are cooking with wine, the alcohol will burn off, giving the final sauce a full, rich flavor.

Roast Duck with Kiwi Sauce

For an elegant dinner, serve this with Wild Rice with Apples and Portobello Mushrooms (page 91), Fresh Pear Salad (page33), and finish with Crème Brulée (page 147).
4 Servings

2 5- to 6-pound **ducks*** (Long Island brand is best)
Salt and freshly ground **black pepper**
1/4 cup **corn oil**

▶ **Preheat** oven to 375 degrees.

▶ Once ducks are defrosted, **remove** giblets. **Rinse** the ducks, **pat dry**, and **sprinkle** with salt and pepper inside and out.

▶ **Heat** oil in deep baking pan and **brown** both sides of the ducks. **Pour** off oil after browned — be careful of hot oil!

▶ **Place** ducks, breast side down, on rack in baking pan and **bake** uncovered for 1-1/2 hours, or until done. When legs pull easily off the breast, the ducks are done.

▶ Ducks may be cooked a day ahead and kept covered in the refrigerator. When ready to serve, **cut** each duck in half, **remove** the back bone, leaving skin and meat intact. Then **cut** into breast, thigh, and leg servings. **Place under broiler** to crisp the ducks.

▶ **Heat** in oven, **serve** on warm plate and **top** with Kiwi Sauce.

* *Since you usually find these frozen, be sure to leave enough time to thaw, according to directions. It's best to thaw poultry slowly in the refrigerator.*

Kiwi Sauce

8 **kiwis**, peeled and finely chopped

1 cup **fresh orange juice**

4 tablespoons **honey**

2 tablespoons **rice vinegar**

1 teaspoon **red pepper flakes**

▶ In a heavy sauce pan, **combine** all ingredients and **cook** over moderate heat until sauce is thickened and has a syrupy consistency. If needed, **thicken** with cornstarch paste.

▶ **Keep warm** or reheat to **serve** with the roasted ducks.

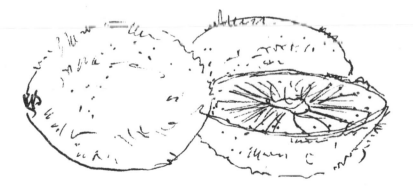

Salmon with Fresh Peach Beurre Blanc
4 Servings

4 7-ounce **salmon filets**, skinned

1 cup **Panko bread crumbs**, found in Asian section of your market

1 teaspoon **seasoned salt** (Montreal seasoning is excellent!)

2 tablespoons **butter**

2 tablespoons **olive oil**

▶ **Mix** bread crumbs and seasoned salt together. **Coat** each piece of salmon on both sides.

▶ **Heat** butter and oil in large skillet and **sauté** salmon filets on both sides until lightly browned.

▶ **Reduce** heat, **cover**, and **cook** for about 15 minutes. When salmon is even color throughout, they are done.

Fresh Peach Beurre Blanc

2 **peaches**, peeled and finely chopped (mangoes are an interesting substitute)

2 tablespoons **sweet wine** such as reisling

2 tablespoons **water**

2 cups dry **white wine**

3 **shallots**, finely chopped

1 cup **butter**, softened

1 teaspoon **salt**

▸ **Sauté** chopped peaches in 2 tablespoons sweet wine and water for 3 minutes. **Drain** and **discard** all but 1/2 cup of the liquid (to correct consistency later).

▸ **Puree** peaches in blender and set aside.

▸ **Cook** 2 cups wine and shallots together over medium high heat until reduced by 3/4. **Transfer** to top of double boiler.

▸ **Add** butter to wine and shallots in small amounts, **mixing** thoroughly with a whisk and continuing to **cook** over low heat until it thickens. If you need to **add** more butter, do so to obtain the consistency of molasses. You may have to remove the pan from the burner — if it gets too hot, the sauce will break down. **Strain** mixture to remove all solids. **Add** salt.

▸ **Add** peaches to the mixture, **stirring** with a wire whisk. Keep sauce **warm** on side of stove, not on burner, until ready to serve.

Sea Scallops on Polenta Cake with Balsamic Caramelized Onion Reduction

This takes a bit of time, but is WELL worth it! You can cook the Caramelized Onions, the reduction, and the Polenta a day or two ahead.
4 Servings

Balsamic Caramelized Onion Reduction

1 cup **balsamic vinegar**
1 tablespoon **sugar**
1 tablespoon **olive oil**
1 tablespoon **butter**
1/2 cup **Caramelized Onions** (page 59)

▸ **Cook** the balsamic vinegar, sugar, olive oil, and butter in a sauce pan over moderate heat until reduced to a syrup consistency, about 15 minutes.

▸ **Combine** vinegar mixture with Caramelized Onions. **Process** in blender and **keep warm** or reheat to serve.

Polenta

1 cup uncooked **polenta** (use 5 minute)
4 cups **water**
2 tablespoons **butter**
1/2 cup **Portobello mushrooms**, sliced
1/2 cup **button mushrooms**, sliced
2 slices **prosciutto**, chopped
1/2 cup **Caramelized Onions** (page 59)
3 tablespoons **Parmesan cheese**
2 **garlic** cloves, minced

▸ **Preheat** oven to 300 degrees.

▸ **Cook** polenta in 4 cups boiling water, **stirring** continually for 10 minutes.

▸ **Heat** butter in skillet and lightly **sauté** mushrooms and prosciutto.

- ▸ **Add** Caramelized Onions, Parmesan cheese, and garlic. **Cook** 2 more minutes.

- ▸ **Fold** mixture into cooked polenta and **cook** 2 more minutes.

- ▸ **Pour** into greased 9x13" pan and **refrigerate** until firm.

- ▸ Just before you are ready to **serve,** cut polenta in desired shapes 1/2" thick (circles, squares or triangles), **sauté** on both sides until nicely browned, then **bake** for 15 minutes or until warm.

Sea Scallops

16 large **sea scallops**, muscles removed
1 tablespoon **seasoned salt** or Montreal seasoning
2 tablespoons **olive oil**
2 tablespoons **butter**
2 cloves **garlic**, minced
1/4 cup **white wine**
3 tablespoons **chopped chives** for garnish

- ▸ **Dust** scallops with seasoned salt or Montreal seasoning.

- ▸ **Heat** olive oil and butter in skillet and **sauté** garlic for 2 minutes.

- ▸ **Add** scallops and **sauté** until browned on both sides.

- ▸ **Add** white wine and **continue cooking** over moderate heat for about 8-10 minutes until done.

To assemble:

- ▸ **Place** shapes of cooked and sautéed polenta on warm plates and **top** with cooked scallops.

- ▸ **Ladle** warm Balsamic Caramelized Onion Reduction over each and **garnish** with chopped chives.

Shrimp Stuffed with Goat Cheese and Tomato Coulis

2-4 Servings

12 **jumbo shrimp**

4 ounces **goat cheese**

4 ounces **cream cheese**

1 clove **garlic**, minced

2 tablespoons **fresh cilantro**, finely chopped

3 teaspoons **heavy cream**

Salt and freshly ground **black pepper** to taste

4 tablespoons melted **butter**

▶ **Preheat** oven to 350 degrees.

▶ **Shell** and devein shrimp, leaving tails attached. **Butterfly** each by slicing down the curve without cutting all the way through. **Flatten** slightly and **set** in ungreased baking pan, cut side up.

▶ **Combine** the goat cheese, cream cheese, garlic, cilantro, and cream in small bowl and **stir** until smooth. **Add** salt and pepper. **Fill** pastry bag with mixture and **set aside**.

▶ **Heat** coulis to serving temperature. **Set out** plates or large shallow soup bowls for serving.

▶ **Drizzle** shrimp with melted butter and **bake** in oven for 3 minutes. **Remove** shrimp and **adjust** oven to 400 degrees.

▶ **Pipe** cheese mixture on top of shrimp and **bake** an additional 4 minutes or until done.

▶ **Spoon** coulis onto serving dishes and **arrange** shrimp on top.

Tomato Coulis

1 tablespoon **olive oil**

4 large **tomatoes**, peeled, seeded and chopped

2 tablespoons **fresh cilantro**, finely chopped

1 tablespoon **jalapeño** or **serrano peppers**, seeded and minced

1 **lime**, juiced

Salt and freshly ground **black pepper** to taste

▸ **Heat** olive oil in frying pan over medium heat. **Add** tomatoes, cover and **simmer** for 5 minutes.

▸ **Add** cilantro and peppers and **cook** uncovered on medium high heat until nearly all moisture has evaporated, 10 to 15 minutes. **Stir** frequently with a whisk to break down larger pieces of tomato.

▸ **Add** lime juice, salt, and pepper. **Keep coulis warm** while preparing prawns or allow to cool and reheat before serving.

Smoked Salmon Cheesecake

A nice summer luncheon idea that's actually better made a day ahead!
10 Servings

2 cups plain **bread crumbs**

1 cup **Parmesan cheese**

4 tablespoons **butter**, melted

1-1/2 pounds **cream cheese**

3 **eggs**

1/2 pound **smoked salmon**, all skin removed, chopped

1/2 pound **Fontina** or **smoked Gouda cheese**, grated

1/2 **red bell pepper**, finely chopped

1/4 cup **red onion**, finely chopped

1 cup **parsley**, finely chopped

1 **shallot**, finely chopped

1/2 teaspoon **salt**

1/2 teaspoon finely ground **black pepper**

Suggested garnishes: **sour cream, capers, chopped hard boiled egg, chopped red onion**

▸ **Preheat** oven to 375 degrees.

▸ **Combine** bread crumbs, Parmesan cheese and melted butter in a small bowl.

▸ **Press** mixture into 10" springform pan, going up the sides of the pan about 1/4".

▸ **Place** spring form pan on cookie sheet and **bake** crust for 15 minutes. Allow to **cool**.

▸ **Soften** cream cheese with electric mixer. Continue mixing on low speed, gradually **add** eggs, and **mix** well.

▸ By hand, **stir** in salmon, cheese, bell pepper, red onion, parsley, shallot, salt and pepper.

▸ **Pour** mixture into crust and **bake** for 45 minutes.

▸ Allow to **cool**, then **refrigerate**. The flavors blend beautifully when you make this a day ahead!

▸ **Garnish** servings with sour cream, capers, chopped egg and red onion. **Serve** warm or at room temperature.

Smoked Salmon Hash with Fresh Chive Cream
6-8 Servings

1/4 cup **fresh chives**, coarsely chopped

2 teaspoons **red wine vinegar**

1 cup **sour cream**

2 teaspoons **fresh lemon juice**

1/2 teaspoon freshly ground **black pepper**

3 large **Yukon Gold potatoes**, skin on, cut in half

1/4 cup **butter**

3 tablespoons **olive oil**

3 **bell peppers**, diced 3/4" pieces — one each yellow, orange, and red add to the eye appeal!

2 small **red onions**, diced in 3/4" pieces

1 cup **Caramelized Onions** (page 59)

2 medium **leeks**, white part only, diced in 3/4" pieces

1 tablespoon each **fresh thyme, oregano,** and **parsley**, chopped

2 tablespoons **fresh Italian parsley**

1 pound **smoked salmon**, skinned and cut into 3/4" pieces

6 stalks **asparagus**, sliced diagonally and blanched

Salt and freshly ground **black pepper** to taste

6 **eggs**, poached at last minute to top each serving

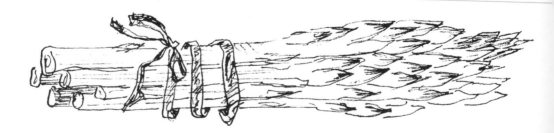

▸ In food processor, **puree** chives with the red wine vinegar.

▸ **Add** sour cream, lemon juice, and pepper and **blend** until smooth.

▸ **Place** in a covered container and **refrigerate** for at least 30 minutes to help the flavors blend. Chive Cream will last up to 3 days in the refrigerator.

▸ **Place** the potatoes in a large sauce pan, **cover** with cold water, cover and bring to a **boil**. **Cook** about 30 minutes until potatoes are just tender, but still firm when tested with a knife. **Drain** and **cool**. When cool enough to handle, **cut** into 3/4" cubes and **set aside**.

▸ **Heat** butter and olive oil in large non-stick skillet over medium heat. **Add** potatoes, bell peppers, red onion, Caramelized Onion, leeks, asparagus, herbs and parsley and **sauté** until potatoes are brown, stirring carefully.

▸ **Add** the smoked salmon and asparagus. **Cook** until the mixture is hot.

▸ As you are cooking the hash, **boil water** for poached eggs.

▸ **Place** servings of hash on warm plates and **top** each with a poached egg.

▸ **Spoon** Chive Cream over the top of each serving.

Stacked Chicken Enchiladas with Pasilla Pepper Sauce

A wonderful south of the border meal that goes well with Jicama Salad (page 36).
6 Servings

2 whole **chicken breasts**, skinned and boned

1/2 cup **canola oil**

2 **white** or **yellow onions**, coarsely chopped

2 cups **Monterey Jack cheese**, grated

2 cups **Cheddar cheese**, grated

12 **corn** or **flour tortillas**

Black beans (optional, page 76)

4 **green onions**, white and part of tops, thinly sliced (optional)

Pasilla Pepper Sauce (recipe follows)

Suggested garnishes: sliced **green onion**, **sour cream**, sliced **avocado**, diced **tomatoes**, and **black olives**

▸ **Preheat** oven to 375 degrees.

▸ **Bake** chicken in foil for 40 minutes. Allow to **cool**, **shred**, and **set aside**.

▸ **Heat** 1/4 cup oil of the oil in a skillet and sauté onions. **Drain** and combine with grated cheeses.

▸ **Add** more oil if needed so bottom of pan is covered. **Heat** oil to medium and **sauté** tortillas one at a time, **remove** from oil, drain, then **dip** in Pasilla Pepper Sauce briefly, **drain** and place one on each of six plates.

▸ When each plate has one cooked tortilla, **place** some chicken and cheese mixture on each, and **top** with a few tablespoons of sauce. You can also **add** black beans and green onions.

▸ **Cook** the remaining tortillas, **placing** one on each stack, then **add** another layer of chicken and cheese then **repeat** cooking tortillas and put another on top of each. Make sure to **dip** each tortilla in the Pasilla Pepper Sauce.

▸ **Warm** the stacked enchiladas in oven for about 15 minutes to melt cheese.

▸ **Garnish** with extra sliced green onion, sour cream, sliced avocados, tomatoes, and black olives.

Pasilla Pepper Sauce

1 **dried pasilla pepper**, whole

1 **jalapeño pepper**, seeded and cut in half

1 small bunch **cilantro**, washed, stemmed and coarsely chopped

1 medium **red onion**, chopped

12 **prunes**, chopped

1/4 cup **raisins**

2 teaspoons **chicken base**

3/4 cup **fresh orange juice**

2 **garlic** cloves, minced

1 13-ounce can **green enchilada sauce**

1 teaspoon ground **cumin**

Salt and freshly ground **black pepper** to taste

- ▸ **Combine** all ingredients in a large sauce pan and **simmer** for one hour. **Taste** and **adjust** seasonings If you want it hotter, add another dried chili or two!

- ▸ If you want a thicker consistency, **add** cornstarch paste and **continue cooking** another 10 minutes.

- ▸ **Process** in food processor, blending until smooth.

- ▸ Keep sauce **warm** while preparing other ingredients.

Stuffed Green Chili Peppers

4 Servings

4 **Anaheim green chili peppers** or poblano chili peppers

6 ounces **goat cheese**, cut in small pieces

1 cup **Fontina cheese**, grated

2 teaspoons **fresh chives**, chopped

3 tablespoons **fresh cilantro**, finely chopped

Salt and freshly ground **black pepper** to taste

1/4 teaspoon **Worcestershire sauce**

1/8 teaspoon **Tabasco sauce**

4 **eggs**, well beaten, on plate

1 cup **corn meal**, on plate

1 tablespoon **bread crumbs**, salt and pepper to taste, mixed with corn meal

1 cup **flour**, on plate

Corn or **canola oil** for frying peppers

1 **avocado**, sliced

1/2 cup **sour cream**

Pasilla Pepper Sauce (page 131)

- ▸ **Preheat** oven to broil.

- ▸ **Broil** whole, washed peppers on cookie sheet, watching closely and rotating often. When they bubble and darken, about 15 minutes, **remove** from oven and place in plastic bag. **Close** bag and allow to sit for one hour.

- ▸ **Slit** each pepper up one side, **peel**, and **remove** seeds. Be careful to keep pepper intact.

- ▸ **Combine** cheeses, chives, cilantro, salt, pepper, Worcestershire and Tabasco sauces to make filling.

- ▸ **Stuff** each pepper with filling, then **roll** in flour, **dip** in egg wash, and **roll** in corn meal mixture to evenly coat each pepper. You may want to **secure** them with toothpicks for the next step!

- ▸ **Heat** oil in skillet and **fry** each pepper until crisp, about 10 minutes.

- ▸ **Garnish** with avocado slices and sour cream and **serve** with Pasilla Chili Sauce.

Variations: *Grind blue flour tortilla chips in the food processor until fine and use in place of bread crumbs. You can add cooked and chopped bacon or prosciutto ham to the filling for a little more body.*

Southwestern Shredded Barbecue Pork

This pork works well in tacos, enchiladas, burritos, and salads. A great buffet dish when served with Spicy Fresh Salsa (page70), Summer White Gazpacho (page 22), and Spicy White Corn with Chilies and Cilantro (page 89).

6-8 Servings

1 5-6 pound **boneless pork butt**

4 tablespoons **seasoned salt** or Montreal Seasoning

1 cup bottled **barbecue sauce**

3 **jalapeño peppers**, seeded, and finely diced

▸ **Preheat** oven to 375 degrees.

▸ **Cut** pork into 4 pieces and **place** in a deep baking pan.

▸ **Combine** seasoning, barbecue sauce and peppers in a small bowl, then **pour** over the pork.

▸ **Cover** pan with foil and **bake** at 375 degrees until tender, about 2-1/2 hours.

▸ **Remove** from oven, **scrape** off excess fat while still warm, and **pull** meat apart with two forks to shred the pork.

▸ **Keep warm** if serving right away or refrigerate.

Swiss Fondue

A fun dish for a light dinner when served with California Orange Salad (page 30).
4 Servings

1 loaf **sourdough bread** cut in 1" cubes

1 clove **garlic**, cut in half

1-1/2 cups **white wine**

1/2 pound **Cheddar cheese**, grated

1/2 pound **Swiss cheese**, grated

2 tablespoons **flour**

Salt and **white pepper** to taste

2 tablespoons **kirsch**

▸ **Preheat** oven to 400 degrees.

▸ **Bake** bread cubes in oven until lightly browned.

▸ **Rub** fondue dish with garlic clove and **discard** garlic.

▸ **Heat** wine in sauce pan. **Combine** cheeses, flour, salt, and pepper and **add** to heated wine. **Add** kirsch and **mix** thoroughly.

▸ **Heat** mixture until cheese is melted, **stirring** frequently.

▸ **Pour** into fondue dish. **Serve** with bread squares.

Variations: *You can use other types of cheese or combinations of Fontina, Gouda, or Gorgonzola. Be sure to cut back on quantities if you use stronger cheeses.*

Texas Chili
10 Servings

2 tablespoons **butter**

2 tablespoons **corn oil**

2 large **sweet onions**, chopped

2 pounds **lean ground beef**

3 cloves **garlic**, minced

1 teaspoon **salt**

2 teaspoons freshly ground **black pepper**

1-1/4 cups **catsup**

1 teaspoon dried, crushed **red chilies**

1 teaspoon **Worcestershire sauce**

3 tablespoons **chili powder** (or more to taste)

1 tablespoon ground **cumin**

1 28-ounce can **diced tomatoes**, with juice

1 28-ounce and 1 15-ounce can **crushed tomatoes**, with juice

1 28-ounce and 1 15-ounce can **pinto beans**, with juice

2 tablespoons **brown sugar**

3 tablespoons **tomato paste**

Suggested garnishes: chopped **onion**, **sour cream**, grated **Cheddar** or **Monterey Jack cheese**, **black olives**.

▸ **Heat** butter and oil in soup pot and **sauté** onions. **Add** ground beef, **cook** through, and **add** garlic, **cooking** another 3 minutes.

▸ **Add** all remaining ingredients and **cook**, stirring often, over medium heat for at least an hour so flavors blend.

▸ **Serve** with a variety of toppings.

Tuna Tortilla Roll with Blue Cheese Dipping Sauce

Fresh fruit makes an excellent side dish for this Marston's favorite!

4 Servings

2 16-ounce cans of **albacore tuna**, drained

1/2 cup **Spicy Fresh Salsa** (page 70)

2 **dill pickles**, finely chopped

1 cup **Cheddar cheese**, grated

1 cup **Monterey Jack** cheese, grated

4 **green onions**, whites and tops, finely sliced

1 cup **mayonnaise**

1 small can **diced green chilies**

4 large **flour tortillas**

2 tablespoons **butter**

2 tablespoons **corn oil**

Otis's Blue Cheese Dressing (page 44)

▶ **Preheat** oven to 400 degrees.

▶ **Mix** tuna, salsa, pickles, cheeses, onions, mayonnaise, and green chilies together.

▶ **Spoon** 1/4 of mixture into each tortilla and **spread** evenly to cover entire surface.

▶ **Roll** up each tortilla and **trim** each end to make them even.

▶ **Heat** butter and oil in frying pan. **Place** tortilla rolls, seam side down, and **cook**, turning until brown on all sides, about 10 minutes.

▶ **Remove** from pan and **bake** for about 15 minutes or microwave until heated through and cheese is melted.

▶ **Serve** with Otis's Blue Cheese Dressing for dipping.

White Lightnin' Chili

A Marston's Restaurant favorite...make it as mild or spicy as you want! This is a fun dish for entertaining when you offer lots of toppings and serve with Jalapeño Corn Bread Bowl (page 83).
10-12 Servings

10 **chicken breast halves**, boned, skinned, cooked (baked or grilled), and cubed or shredded

1/4 cup **olive oil**

2 tablespoons **butter**

2 large **onions**, finely chopped

3 cloves **garlic**, minced

2 pounds **small white beans** (washed and checked for pebbles)

2 tablespoons **chicken base**

3 quarts **water**

1 tablespoon ground **cumin**

3 teaspoons dried **oregano**

1/4 teaspoon ground **cloves**

1 8-ounce can **green chilies**, diced

2 **jalapeño peppers**, seeded and diced (add up to 4 for spicier chili)

Suggested garnishes: grated **Monterey Jack** cheese, diced **avocados, sour cream, tortilla chips** or **Crispy Tortilla Strips** (page 3), **Spicy Fresh Salsa** (page 70), diced **tomatillos**

▶ **Bake** chicken breasts in foil for about 40 minutes or **grill** on the barbecue. Grilling gives the chicken a wonderful flavor! You can grill the peppers, too, which takes about 5 minutes. (If you wish to cook chicken with bean mixture, you can cut it into cubes before adding to water. **Add** in the last half hour of cooking time for beans.)

▶ **Heat** olive oil and butter in large soup pot and **sauté** onions and garlic for about 10 minutes over medium heat.

▶ **Add** beans, chicken base, and water (should cover beans by 2″). Bring to a **boil**, **reduce** heat slightly to a low boil, cover, and **cook** for one hour, until beans are tender.

▶ **Add** cumin, oregano, cloves, chilies, and peppers and **cook** an additional 10 minutes.

▶ **Cut** chicken in small pieces, **add** it to the chili and **continue cooking** about 15 minutes.

▶ **Ladle** into soup bowls and **serve** with a variety of chili toppings.

A tip from Otis...
I like to use both butter and oil to sauté vegetables. The combination prevents the butter from burning.

Desserts

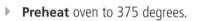

Belgian Chocolate Soufflé
Elegant individual soufflés for a memorable ending to a special dinner party!
6 Servings

15 **eggs**

1 pound **semi-sweet Belgian chocolate**

1 cup **whipping cream**

2 tablespoons **butter**, melted

1 tablespoon **Grand Marnier**

1/4 cup **powdered sugar**

▶ **Preheat** oven to 375 degrees.

▶ **Separate** eggs, beat yolks, and **set aside**.

▶ **Beat** egg whites until stiff and **set aside**.

▶ **Melt** chocolate in top of a double boiler. **Reserve** 1/2 cup for the sauce. **Allow** melted chocolate to **cool**.

▶ In large bowl, **mix** beaten egg yolks with cooled melted chocolate, then **fold** in egg whites carefully with a rubber spatula, so chocolate color is even.

▶ **Pour** into greased and sugared 6-ounce ramekins, filling each about 3/4 full.

▶ **Bake** for 30 minutes.

▶ For sauce, **combine** whipping cream, melted butter and 1/2 cup reserved melted chocolate, and Grand Marnier in a heavy saucepan.

▶ Just before soufflés are ready to come out of the oven, **cook** sauce slowly over medium heat until warm.

▶ **Puncture** top of soufflés and **spoon** sauce into hot soufflés; **garnish** with powdered sugar and **serve** immediately.

Bread Pudding with Apricot Grand Marnier Sauce

An old-fashioned favorite...updated and with a surprise topping!
8 Servings

6 cups **whipping cream**

1 pint **half and half**

1 whole **egg**

6 **egg yolks**

8 tablespoons **sugar**

1 tablespoon **vanilla extract**

8 **breakfast bear claws**, broken in pieces (Svenhards brand are good, but any variety is fine)

1/4 cup **raisins**

Suggested garnishes: fresh **whipped cream** and fresh ground **nutmeg**

▶ **Preheat** oven to 375 degrees.

▶ **Combine** all ingredients except bear claws and raisins, **mixing** thoroughly for the custard.

▶ **Sprinkle** raisins in 9x13" baking pan with 4-inch sides. **Cover** with pieces of bear claw.

▶ **Pour** custard over the bear claws and **cover** with foil.

▶ **Place** baking pan in a larger pan filled with warm water half way up the outside. **Bake**, covered, for 45-60 minutes, **checking** after about 30 minutes. The custard should be somewhat soft, not real firm.

▶ **Serve** warm with Apricot Grand Marnier Sauce, whipped cream, and a dash of nutmeg.

Apricot Grand Marnier Sauce

3 tablespoons **Grand Marnier**

1 16-ounce jar **apricot preserves**

▶ **Combine** both ingredients in food processor and **mix** until smooth.

Chocolate Royale

This was one of Jean Marston's favorite "special occasion" recipes.
12 Servings

Pecan Mixture

1/2 cup **butter**

1 cup **powdered sugar**

3 **egg yolks**, beaten

3 **egg whites**, beaten in peaks

1 cup chopped **pecans**

▸ **Cream** butter and sugar, **add** egg yolks and pecans.

▸ **Fold** in egg whites and **set aside**.

Cocoa Mixture

3 **egg yolks**, beaten

1/2 cup **cocoa**

1-1/2 cups **powdered sugar**

4 tablespoons **boiling water**

1 tablespoon **vanilla**

3 **egg whites**, beaten in peaks

Crust

40 **vanilla wafers,** crushed

Suggested garnishes: 1/2 cup chopped **pecans**, **whipped cream**, **mint leaves**

▸ **Mix** egg yolks, cocoa, powdered sugar, and boiling water.

▸ **Add** vanilla and fold in egg whites. **Set aside**.

To assemble:

▸ **Cover** the bottom of a 9x13" baking pan with 1/3 of the vanilla wafers.

▸ **Pour** 1/3 of cocoa mixture on top of crust.

▸ **Sprinkle** 1/3 of pecan mixture on top of cocoa mixture.

▸ **Repeat** layers of wafers, cocoa mixture, and pecan mixture two more times.

▸ **Sprinkle** top with 1/2 cup chopped pecans.

▸ **Refrigerate** for 24 hours.

Serve in squares topped with whipped cream and mint leaf.

Note: *Since you are not cooking the eggs, be sure they are fresh and well refrigerated.*

Chocolate Crème Brulée

A chocolate version of Marston's most popular dessert.
8 Servings

5 **egg yolks**

1 quart **whipping cream**

5 tablespoons **sugar**

1 tablespoon **vanilla**

3 tablespoons **Suisse Mocha International Coffee** (General Foods, found in coffee section)

5 ounces **Belgian chocolate** (may substitute Ghirardelli's dark chocolate chips)

1/4 cup **milk**, warmed

Garnish: whipped cream and finely chopped **Marston's Candied Pecans** (page 64)

▶ **Preheat** oven to 375 degrees.

▶ **Combine** egg yolks, whipping cream, sugar, vanilla and coffee in a large bowl. **Whip** together until blended.

▶ **Pour** into 8-ounce custard cups and **place** in baking pan. **Fill** pan with water halfway up sides of cups. **Bake** in water bath for 45-60 minutes, until custard is firm.

▶ **Place** in refrigerator to cool.

▶ **Melt** chocolate in top of double boiler. **Add** warmed milk, **stirring** frequently to **mix** and heat thoroughly.

▶ **Pour** a thin layer of chocolate on top of each cooked crème brulée, covering completely, and **refrigerate** overnight.

▶ **Serve** topped with fresh whipped cream and Marston's Candied Pecans.

Note: *For a list of distributors of Marston's Candied Pecans and other products, go to* **marstonproducts.com**.

Crème Brulée

The hallmark dessert at Marston's.
8 Servings

5 **egg yolks**
1 quart **whipping cream**
6 tablespoons **sugar**
1 tablespoon **vanilla**
8 tablespoons **brown sugar**

▸ **Preheat** oven to 375 degrees.

▸ **Combine** egg yolks, whipping cream, sugar, and vanilla in a large bowl and **whip** together by hand until blended.

▸ **Pour** into 8-ounce custard cups and place in baking pan. **Fill** pan with water halfway up sides of cups.

▸ **Bake** in water bath for 45-60 minutes, until custard is firm.

▸ **Refrigerate** overnight.

▸ **Sprinkle** a tablespoon of brown sugar over each custard, covering the top completely, and **heat** under broiler, watching closely, until caramelized, about 3 minutes.

Note: *You can freeze crème brulée up to two weeks. Thaw before serving.*

Frozen Pumpkin Praline Torte

A perfect holiday dessert that you can make 2 to 3 days in advance!
6 Servings

Crust

1 quart **praline ice cream**, softened

Filling

2 cups **whipping cream**

1 16-ounce can of **pumpkin**

1-1/2 cups **sugar**

2-1/2 teaspoons **cinnamon**

2 teaspoons ground **nutmeg**

1/2 teaspoon **salt**

Sauce

1/4 cup **light brown sugar**, packed

2 tablespoons **butter**

1 tablespoon **water**

1 cup **Marston's Candied Pecans** (page64)

- ▶ **Freeze** an 8-inch spring form pan for at least 30 minutes.

- ▶ **Spoon** softened ice cream into pan, **press** into bottom and half way up the sides. **Place** plastic wrap over ice cream and gently **press** down to even 1/2" thickness. **Leave** plastic wrap on as cover and **freeze** for 2 hours or overnight.

- ▶ **Whip** 2 cups of whipping cream until stiff and **set aside** in refrigerator. If making ahead, only whip 1-3/4 cups of the cream now, reserving remainder for topping just before serving.

- ▶ In saucepan, **combine** pumpkin, sugar, cinnamon, nutmeg and salt. **Heat** over medium heat until blended. **Remove** from heat and allow to **cool** for one hour.

- ▶ **Combine** pumpkin mixture with 1-1/2 cups of the whipped cream.

- ▶ **Remove** pan from freezer, **remove** plastic wrap and **spread** pumpkin mixture evenly into crust. **Cover** with plastic wrap and **freeze** overnight.

- ▶ Before serving, **combine** brown sugar, butter and water in small saucepan and **boil** over medium heat until thickened and golden brown. **Add** candied pecans.

- ▶ When ready to serve, **remove** torte from freezer, **unmold** and **place** portions on plates. **Top** with the pecan sauce or **drizzle** sauce on plate around the torte. **Garnish** with a dollop of whipped cream.

Note: *For a list of distributors of Marston's Candied Pecans and other products, go to* **marstonproducts.com**.

Gingerbread with Orange Sauce and Lemon Whipped Cream

Comfort food to warm the heart and soul!
6 Servings

1 box **gingerbread mix**
1 **orange**, juiced
2 tablespoons **sugar**
2 tablespoons **water**
2 tablespoons **cornstarch**
1 cup **whipping cream**
2 tablespoons **powdered sugar**
1 teaspoon **fresh lemon juice**
1 teaspoon **lemon zest**
6 fresh **mint leaves**
1 teaspoon **orange zest**

▸ **Bake** gingerbread according to directions in loaf pan and set aside.

▸ To make the orange sauce, **heat** fresh orange juice, sugar, and water. **Stir** over medium heat and **add** cornstarch a teaspoon at a time until nearly syrup consistency. **Strain** mixture and **set aside**. **Keep warm** if serving right away or reheat just before serving.

▸ **Whip** cream. **Add** powdered sugar, lemon juice, and lemon zest.

▸ **Spoon** orange sauce onto plates, **place** a piece of warm gingerbread atop the sauce and **garnish** with whipped cream, fresh mint leaf, and a sprinkle of orange zest.

Key Lime Pie

6-8 servings

8 ounces **unsalted butter**

5 **egg yolks**, beaten

1/2 cup plus 3 tablespoons **sugar**

3/4 cup **fresh lime juice** (use key limes if you can find them)

2 tablespoons **unflavored gelatin** mixed with 1 tablespoon **water**

1 teaspoon **green food coloring**

1 pint of **whipping cream**

1/2 cup sweet **shredded coconut**

Zest of one **lime**

8 thin slices of **lime** for garnish

1 **pastry** or **graham cracker pie shell** (homemade or store bought)

▸ **Melt** butter in double boiler over medium heat. Add egg yolks and 1/2 cup sugar and cook, stirring with wire whisk for 3 minutes.

▸ **Add** lime juice and cook, **stirring** continually so eggs don't set up, another 10 minutes until mixture starts to thicken.

▸ When mixture thickens, **remove** from heat and **taste, adding** more lime juice or sugar to suit your taste. **Strain** to remove any egg particles. **Blend** in gelatin/water mixture and food coloring and **refrigerate**.

▸ **Whip** 1-1/2 cups of the cream until stiff and **fold in** 3 tablespoons of sugar. **Fold** the whipped cream into cooled lime mixture, **blending** well.

▸ **Pour** mixture into pie shell and **smooth** top with a spatula. **Sprinkle** lime zest over top of pie, **cover** and **refrigerate** for 24 hours.

▸ **To serve, whip** remaining cream with the sweet shredded coconut. **Top** each slice with coconut whipped cream and **garnish** with a slice of lime.

Lemon Curd Tart with Fresh Berries

This recipe came from our English friend, Vivi, who shared her secret for a true English lemon curd.
8 Servings

5 **egg yolks**

8 ounces **unsalted butter**

4 tablespoons **sugar**

3/4 cup fresh **lemon juice**

Pastry tart

1 cup **whipping cream**, whipped

2 cups **fresh berries**

▸ **Combine** egg yolks, butter, and sugar in the top of a double boiler. Cook over medium heat, stirring with a wire whisk until it starts to thicken. Do not let it boil.

▸ **Add** lemon juice, a little at a time, stirring constantly. **Continue cooking** over medium-low heat, **stirring** frequently, for about 10-15 minutes.

▸ **Remove** from heat and **strain** to remove any cooked egg particles. **Let cool**.

▸ **Spoon** one recipe of lemon curd into pastry tart, **top** with whipped cream and **sprinkle** berries or other fresh fruit over the top.

Lemon Curd Angel Dessert

1 cup **whipping cream**

2 tablespoons **sugar**

1 recipe **lemon curd**

1 8-12 ounce **angel food cake** (home or bakery made)

3 baskets **fresh berries** (Use whatever is in season...this dessert is great with a mix of blueberries, blackberries, and strawberries!)

▸ **Whip** cream with sugar; **fold in** lemon curd.

▸ **Slice** cake in 3 layers. **Alternate** layers of cake, lemon curd, and berries.

▸ **Frost** entire cake with lemon curd mix and **top** with a handful of berries.

Warm Chocolate Cakelettes

This dessert will warm the cockles of anyone's heart!
4 Servings

4 ounces **butter**

9 ounces **bittersweet chocolate** (Valrhona is excellent; Ghirardelli's is good, too)

2 **eggs**

2 **egg yolks**

1/4 cup **sugar**

1 pinch **salt**

2 tablespoons **flour**

Vanilla bean, coffee, or **peppermint stick ice cream**

Suggested garnishes: **fresh berries, fresh mint leaves, powdered sugar**

▷ **Preheat** oven to 425 degrees.

▷ **Spray** four 6-ounce ramekins or dessert molds with cooking spray and set on a baking sheet.

▷ In a double boiler, over simmering water, **melt** the butter and 6 ounces of the chocolate. **Reserve** remaining chocolate for topping.

▷ Using an electric mixer, **beat** eggs, yolks, sugar, and salt at high speed until thickened and pale.

▷ **Whisk** the chocolate until smooth and quickly **fold** it into the egg mixture, **adding** the flour.

▷ **Spoon** the batter into the prepared ramekins and **bake** for 12 minutes, until the sides of the cakes are firm but the centers are still soft. Let the cakes **cool** in the ramekins for one minute, then **cover** each with an inverted dessert plate. Carefully **turn** each one over, **let stand** for 10 seconds and then **unmold**.

▷ **Melt** remaining chocolate in the double boiler. **Drizzle** a portion over and around each cake.

▷ **Place** two small scoops of ice cream next to each cake and **garnish** with a mint leaf and/or fresh berries. **Sprinkle** powdered sugar over each plate and **serve** warm.

Note: *Cake batter can be refrigerated for several hours. Bring to room temperature before baking.*

Menus

While managing the kitchen at Marston's, Otis and Sally planned menus and cooked for private parties, Friday night dinners, and seasonal celebrations. Here are some of their favorite menus. *Denotes recipes in this book.

Brunch Buffet
Marston's Fantastic French Toast*
Served with warm maple syrup, Banana Sauté*, powdered sugar, fresh berries, and lemon wedges.
Platter of grilled Canadian bacon, chicken cilantro sausage, and brown sugar cured bacon
Smoked Salmon Hash with Fresh Chive Cream*
Sliced seasonal fresh fruits topped with diced fresh mint
Fresh orange juice

Saturday Morning Breakfast
Spicy tomato juice with celery stir stick
Corned Beef Hash topped with Poached Eggs*
Fresh orange slice garnish
Basket of warm bread

Luncheons
Otis's Blackened Salmon Caesar Salad*
Cheddar Cheese Popovers*
Chocolate Crème Brulée*

Marston's Restaurant Favorite
California Orange Salad*
Cheddar Cheese Popovers*
Bread Pudding with Apricot Grand Marnier Sauce* and Whipped Cream

Grilled Lamb Loin Salad with Rosemary Balsamic Vinaigrette*
Beer Cheese Crostini*
Lemon Curd Tart with Fresh Berries*

Cream of Tomato Dill Soup *
Cordierra Salad with Grilled Chicken*
Key Lime Pie*

Crab Capellini with Honey Mustard Sauce*
Jicama Salad with Sliced Avocado*
Crème Brulée*

▼

Split Pea Soup with Ham and Andouille Sausage*
Tuna Tortilla Roll with Blue Cheese Dipping Sauce*
Fresh Fruit

▼

Clam Chowder in a Bread Bowl*
Otis's Caesar Salad*

▼

Potato Cheese Leek Soup*
Arugula Salad with Balsamic Mustard Vinaigrette*
Cheesy Garlic Bread*

Dinners

Otis's Meatloaf with Tomato Barbecue Sauce*
Fresh Spinach Mashed Potatoes*
Grilled Vegetables*
Caesar Salad*
Warm Gingerbread with Orange Sauce and Lemon Whipped Cream*

▼

Roasted Red Bell Pepper Soup*
Filet Mignon with Portobello Mushroom Sauce*
Watercress and Oak Leaf Lettuce Salad with Champagne Grapes*
Swiss Scalloped Yams*
Belgian Chocolate Soufflé*

▼

Summer White Gazpacho*
Stuffed Green Chili Peppers* topped with Crispy Tortilla Strips*
Black Beans*
Jalapeño Corn Bread*
Spicy Fresh Salsa*
Crème Brulée*

▼

Cream of Zucchini and Green Pea Soup*
Fresh Pear Salad*
Spicy White Corn with Cilantro*
Macadamia Encrusted White Fish with Mango Mayonnaise*
Warm Chocolate Cakelettes*

▼

French Onion Soup with Otis's Fresh Baked Rye Croutons*
Fresh Fig and Gorgonzola Salad*
Roast Duck with Kiwi Sauce*
Wild Rice with Apples and Portobello Mushrooms*
Fresh Asparagus
Frozen Pumpkin Praline Torte*

▼

California Orange Salad* (omit chicken and blue cheese)
Herb Crusted Rosemary Pork Roulade*
Onion Marmalade*
Grilled Asparagus
Swiss Scalloped Yams*
Gingerbread with Orange Sauce and Lemon Whipped Cream*

▼

Chicken Lime Vegetable Soup*
Spinach Salad*
Crispy Salmon with Shallot Caper Sauce*
Fresh Corn Succotash*
Garlic Mashed Potatoes*
Lemon Curd Tart with Fresh Berries*

California Backyard Barbecue Buffet
Jicama Salad*
Platter of red and yellow tomatoes and sliced mozzarella drizzled with Otis's Fabulous Dressing* and chopped fresh basil
Black Beans and Rice*
Spicy White Corn with Cilantro*
Guacamole*
Spicy Fresh Salsa*
Baby Back Ribs Texas Style *
Southwestern Shredded Barbecue Pork*
Texas Chili*
Basket of warm corn and flour tortillas
Jalapeño Corn Bread Bowl*
Chocolate Royale*

Index

Recipes in bold indicate dishes served at Marston's Restaurant.

INDEX ■ 157

Recipes in bold indicate dishes served at Marston's Restaurant.

'ecipes in bold indicate dishes served at Marston's Restaurant.

Tips from Otis

To order Marston's Candied Pecans, Marston's San Pasqual Dressing, *Homestyle Elegance*, or other products, visit our website at
marstonproducts.com

Recipes in bold indicate dishes served at Marston's Restaurant.